Just for the Lower Level ISEE

- **Test Prep Works materials are developed for a specific test and level, making it easier for students to focus on relevant content**

- **The Lower Level ISEE is for students applying for admission to grades 5-6 – see table at the end of this book for materials for other grades**

- **Three books are available from Test Prep Works to help students prepare for the Lower Level ISEE**

Success on the Lower Level ISEE: A Complete Course

- Strategies for each section of the test
- Reading and vocabulary drills
- In-depth math content instruction with practice sets
- 1 full-length practice test

30 Days to Acing the Lower Level ISEE

- Strategies for each section of the test
- Fifteen "workouts", each providing practice problems and detailed explanations for every section of the test
- Perfect for additional practice or homework

The Best Unofficial Practice Tests for the Lower Level ISEE

- 2 additional full-length practice tests

TEST PREP WORKS, LLC.

Are you an educator?

Incorporate materials from Test Prep Works into your test prep program

- Use the materials developed specifically for the test and level your students are taking

- Customize our books to fit your program

    - Choose content modules from any of our books – even from multiple books

    - Add your branding to the cover and title page

    - Greet your students with an introductory message

    - Create custom books with a one-time setup fee[1], then order copies at list price[2] with no minimum quantities

- Volume discounts available for bulk orders of 50+ copies

You provide the expertise – let us provide the materials

Contact *sales@testprepworks.com* for more info

1 - Setup fees start at $199 per title, which includes branding of the cover and title page and a customer-provided introductory message. Additional customization will incur additional setup fees.

2 - The list price for custom books is the same as the list price of the corresponding title available for retail sale. If the content of a book is modified so that it no longer corresponds to a book available for retail sale, then Test Prep Works will set the list price prior to assessing any setup fees.

TEST PREP WORKS, LLC.

SUCCESS

ON THE **Lower Level ISEE**

A Complete Course

Christa Abbott, M.Ed.

Published by:
Test Prep Works, LLC
PO Box 100572
Arlington, VA 22210
www.TestPrepWorks.com

For information about buying this title in bulk, or for editions with customized covers or content, please contact us at sales@testprepworks.com or (703) 944-6727.

The ISEE is a registered trademark of the ERB. They have not endorsed nor are they associated in any way with this book.

Neither the author nor the publisher of this book claims responsibility for the accuracy of this book or the outcome of students who use these materials.

ISBN: 978-1-939090-03-4

Contents

Quantitative Reasoning and Mathematics Achievement

Quantitative Sections- Basic Strategies

Math Content Sections

Whole Numbers on the ISEE

Fractions, Decimals, and Percents

Algebra

About the Author

Christa Abbott has been a private test prep tutor for over a decade. She has worked with students who have been admitted to and attended some of the top independent schools in the country. Over the years, she has developed materials for each test that truly make the difference.

Christa is a graduate of Middlebury College and received her Masters in Education from the University of Virginia, a program nationally known for its excellence. Her background in education allows her to develop materials based on the latest research about how we learn so that preparation can be an effective and efficient use of time. Her materials are also designed to be developmentally appropriate for the ages of the students taking the tests. In her free time, she enjoys hiking, tennis, Scrabble, and reading. Her greatest joy is spending time with her husband and three children.

Christa continues to work with students one-on-one in the Washington, D.C., area. She also works with students internationally via Skype. If you are interested in these services, please visit www.ChristaAbbott.com.

About Test Prep Works, LLC

Test Prep Works, LLC, was founded to provide effective materials for test preparation. Its founder, Christa Abbott, spent years looking for effective materials for the private school entrance  exams but came up empty-handed. The books available combined several different tests and while there are overlaps, they are not the same test. Christa found this to be very, very overwhelming for students who were in Elementary and Middle School and that just didn't seem necessary. Christa developed her own materials to use with students that are specific for each level of the test and are not just adapted from other books. For the first time, these materials are available to the general public as well as other tutors. Please visit www.TestPrepWorks.com to view a complete array of offerings as well as sign up for a newsletter with recent news and developments in the world of admissions and test preparation.

Notes for Parents

What is the ISEE?

ISEE stands for Independent School Entrance Exam. It is published by the Education Records Bureau (ERB). If you have students already in independent school, you may have seen ERB scores before. You may also have heard of another independent school entrance exam- the SSAT. The schools that your student is applying to may accept either the SSAT or the ISEE, or they may exclusively use one test or the other. It can also depend upon what grade your child is applying for. Contact each school to which your child will apply to be sure that he or she is taking the correct test.

- Contact schools so that your child takes the right test

What level should I register my child for?

This book is designed to help students who are taking the Lower Level ISEE. If students are applying for grade 5 or grade 6, then they should be taking the Lower Level ISEE. If this does not describe your student, please visit www.TestPrepWorks.com to order the correct materials for the level that your student will be taking.

- Lower Level is for students applying to grade 5 or grade 6

What do I need to know about registering my child?

The most important fact that families need to know is that a child can only take the test once in a six-month period. Do not have your child take the test "just to see how he does" because he will not be able to take the test again in the same admissions season!

- Students can only take the test once in each admissions season, or six month period

Registration is done through the ERB. Their website is www.erblearn.org. On this site, you can also download a copy of *What to Expect on the ISEE*. The beginning of the book gives some sample problems and the end of the book has a partial practice test. I would recommend that you wait to give your student this practice test until after he or she has completed other preparations. Practice tests from the actual writers of the test are a valuable commodity, so save the practice test from *What to Expect on the ISEE*.

- Download *What to Expect on the ISEE*
- Feel free to have your student work through sample problems in the beginning of the book, just save the practice test for after your student has done other preparations

The test can be taken in a paper form or online at a testing center. The paper format is given at a number of schools in a large group setting. It can also be given in a small group setting at the ERB's New York offices or at a very limited number of sites in other locations. In the most recent ISEE student guide, small group testing sites are listed for Connecticut, Florida, Massachusetts, New York, Pennsylvania, Texas, China, South Korea, and Turkey. Outside of these areas, small group testing with the paper form is not available.

- Most students take the paper format at a school in a large group setting
- A very limited number of sites give the paper test in a small group setting- the list of these sites is in the ISEE Student Guide

Students can also take a computer-based form of the test at Prometric centers nationwide. The test is the exact same as the paper format test. Students can still go back and change answers. The only difference is that the students who take the computer-based test get to type their essay but students who take the paper form have to handwrite their essays. If you do go the testing center route, just make sure that your student knows that there will be people of all ages there taking a variety of tests. You can choose the time and date that works best for your student if you go the computer-based route.

- The ISEE can be taken at a testing center on the computer
- The computer-based test offers flexibility with date/time

You must request accommodations if your child needs them. If your child has an IEP or receives accommodations in school, then start the paperwork with the ERB promptly. Don't wait until the last minute as this is very stress inducing for both you and your student. If your child is going to get extended time, he or she should know that as he or she works through practice sections. Also, since your child can only take the ISEE once per admissions season, you won't have a "do over" if your child takes the test without accommodations.

Just how important is the ISEE to the admissions process?

Every school uses the test differently. In general, the more competitive the school, the more test scores are going to matter, but there are certainly exceptions to that rule. Reading through a school's literature is a great way to figure out whether or not a school emphasizes or deemphasizes testing. Also, call the admissions office where your child will be applying. Admissions officers are often quite candid about what the testing profile of their admitted students tends to be.

- Talk to the schools that your child is applying to in order to get a sense of the scores they look for

How can I help my student?

Keep your own cool. Never once has a student gotten a higher score because mom or dad freaked out. Approach this as a project. Good test taking skills can be learned and by working through the process with your child in a constructive manner, you are providing them with a roadmap for how to approach challenges in the future. We want them to be confident, but to earn that confidence through analysis, self-monitoring, and practice.

- Keep a positive attitude

What are the key elements of successful test preparation?

Analysis

It is important that students don't just do practice problem after practice problem without figuring out what they missed, and most importantly, WHY they missed those problems. Is there a particular type of problem that they keep missing? One issue that many students have is categorizing problems. When you go through a problem that your student is stuck on, be sure to point out the words in the problem that pointed you in the correct direction.

- Teach your child to analyze why he or she missed a question

Self-monitoring

Students should develop a sense of their strengths and weaknesses so that they can best focus preparation time. This book provides many practice opportunities for each section, but your child may not need that. For example, if they are acing the math problems, they shouldn't keep spending valuable time doing more of those problems. Maybe their time would be better spent on vocabulary. This is a great opportunity, and your student is at the perfect age, to be learning how to prioritize.

- Help your student prioritize material to work on

Practice

While it is important that a student understand WHY he is doing what he is doing, at a certain point it just needs to become automatic. This is a timed test and you want the strategies to spring to mind without having to reinvent the wheel every time. Practice will make this process fast and easy. On test day all that practice will kick in to make this a positive and affirming experience for your student.

- Teach your child that he or she needs to practice what they have learned so that it is automatic on test day

How To Use This Book

This book is designed to teach you what you need to know in order to maximize your Lower Level ISEE performance.

There are strategies for each of the four multiple-choice sections as well as advice on the writing section.

This book also includes a lot of content practice. There is a complete vocabulary section and detailed instruction for the math concepts that are tested on the ISEE.

You may find that you don't need to complete all of the content instruction. It is important to prioritize your time! If vocabulary is a weakness for you, then spend your time working through the vocabulary lessons. If some of the math concepts are challenging, then you should spend your study time working through the math sections.

At the end of this book is a practice test. This will give you a good idea of how you are doing with timing and what it feels like to take a longer test. There are included score charts, but please keep in mind that these are a very rough estimate. It is very, very tough to accurately determine percentiles without a huge amount of data, so we have included percentiles just as a rough guideline of how the scoring works.

There is additional practice available once you complete the practice test in this book. Test Prep Works has published another book, *The Best Unofficial Practice Tests for the Lower Level ISEE*, with two additional full-length practice tests. Also, be sure complete the practice test in *What to Expect on the ISEE* (available at www.erblearn.org). That will give you your best estimate of performance on the actual ISEE.

I have spent years studying the test and analyzing the different question types, content, and the types of answers that the test writers prefer. Now you can benefit from my hard work! I will show how to approach questions so that you can raise your score significantly.

Let's get started!

The Format of the Lower Level ISEE

You can expect to see four scored sections plus an essay. The sections are listed below in the order that they will appear on the ISEE. One great thing about the ISEE is that it has a very predictable format.

The Four Scored Sections

- ✓ Verbal Reasoning
    - 17 vocabulary questions
    - 17 sentence completion questions

- ✓ Quantitative Reasoning
    - 38 math word problems
    - Less focused on calculations and equations, more focused on thinking through a problem

- ✓ Reading Comprehension
    - 25 total questions
    - 5 passages, each with 5 questions about it

- ✓ Mathematics Achievement
    - 30 math questions
    - More focused on calculations and knowing specific math terminology

The Essay

- Prompt for students to respond to
- 30 minutes to complete
- Two lined pieces of paper to write response on
- NOT scored, but a copy of the essay is sent to schools that student applies to

Now, on to the strategies and content! The strategies covered in this book will focus on the multiple-choice sections since those are what is used to determine your score. Please also see the essay section for tips on how to write the essay.

What Students Need To Know For the ISEE- Just the Basics

Here is what you really need to know to do well on the Lower Level ISEE:

How the Scoring Works

On the ISEE, your score is determined just by how many questions you answer correctly. They do not take off any points if you answer a question incorrectly.

When To Guess

On the ISEE, you want to answer absolutely everything, even if you haven't even looked at the question. You may answer the question correctly and they don't take off any points for questions that you answer incorrectly. If you are running out of time or don't understand a question, just blindly guess- you may choose the right answer!

The Percentile Score

You will get a raw score for the ISEE based upon how many you get right or wrong. This raw score will then be converted into a scaled score. Neither of these scores is what schools are really looking at. They are looking for your percentile scores.

Percentile score is what schools are really looking at

The percentile score compares you to other students that are in your grade. For example, let's say that you are an eighth grader and you scored in the 70th percentile. What this means is that out of a hundred students in your grade, you would have done better than 70 of them.

- Your percentile score compares you only to other students in your grade

Many students applying to independent schools are used to getting almost all the questions correct on a test. You will probably miss more questions on this test than you are used to missing, but because the percentile score is what schools are looking at, don't let it get to you.

- You may miss more questions than you are used to, but that is OK as long as other students your age miss those questions

You should also look at the scoring charts in *What to Expect on the ISEE*. These charts will give you a rough idea of how many questions you need to answer correctly in order to achieve different percentile scores.

Students always want to know, "What is a good percentile score?" Well, that depends on what school you are applying to. The best resource is the admissions officers at the schools that you want to attend.

The Mother of All Strategies

Use the Process of Elimination, or "Ruling Out"

If you remember nothing else on test day, remember to use the process of elimination. This is a multiple-choice test, and there are often answers that don't even make sense.

When you read a question, you want to read all of the answer choices before selecting one. You need to keep in mind that the test will ask you to choose the answer choice that "best" answers the question. Best is a relative word, so how can you know which answer choice best answers the question if you don't read them all?

- After you read the question, read ALL of the answer choices
- Look for the "best" answer, which may just be the least wrong answer choice

After you have read all of the answer choices, rule them out in order from most wrong to least wrong. Sometimes the "best" answer choice is not a great fit, but it is better than the others. This process will also clarify your thinking so that by the time you get down to only two answer choices, you have a better idea of what makes choices right or wrong.

- Rule out in order from most wrong to least wrong

On the ISEE, they don't take off for wrong answer choices, so it can be tempting to just blindly guess if you are confused. However, put a little of work into the question before you do that. Even if you are having trouble understanding a question, there may be one or two answer choices that don't even make sense.

- Use ruling out before you guess, even if the question leaves you totally confused

Verbal Section- Basic Strategies

In the verbal section you will see two question types:

- Synonyms
- Sentence completions

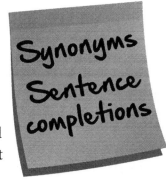

On the synonym questions, you will be given one question word and then you have to choose the answer choice that has the word that comes closest in meaning to that question word.

Synonym questions look something like this:

1. JOYOUS:
   (A) crying
   (B) happy
   (C) loud
   (D) mad

Out of all the answer choice words, happy comes closest in meaning to joyous. Choice B is correct.

The synonym questions won't all be that easy, but you get the idea.

The sentence completion questions give you a sentence where a dashed line has replaced one or more words. Your job is to figure out which answer choice should be inserted instead of that dashed line so that the sentence makes sense.

The sentence completion questions usually look something like this:

2. The student was afraid that she had not done well on the test, but when she got her scores back she was pleasantly -------.
    (A) boisterous
    (B) panicked
    (C) surprised
    (D) worried

In this case, the beginning of the sentence tells us that the student thinks she hasn't done well. We then have the conjunction "but" which tells us that the second part of the sentence will contradict the first, so something good must have happened. Choice C fits the bill and it is the correct answer choice.

There can also be sentence completion questions where we have to choose which phrase would best complete the sentence rather than just filling in a word. The key to these questions is to stick to the main idea of the half of the sentence that we are given.

Here is an example of this type of question:

3. At top of the roller coaster, the children -------.
    (A) went to their next class
    (B) got dressed for the day
    (C) squealed with delight
    (D) finished their lunches

What is the first part of the sentence talking about? It is talking about being at the top of a roller coaster. Would it make sense to go to a class, get dressed for the day, or finish your lunch at the top of a roller coaster? No. But it would make sense to squeal with delight. Answer choice C is correct.

These are the basic question types that you will see in the Verbal Reasoning section. They are very different, so we have different strategies for each question type.

Synonym Strategies

There are several strategies that we can use on the synonyms section. Which strategy you use for an individual question is up to you. It depends on what roots you know, whether or not you have heard the word before, and your gut sense about a word.

Think of these strategies as being your toolbox. Several tools can get the job done.

Here are the strategies:

- Come up with your own word
- Using positive or negative
- Use context
- Look for roots or word parts that you know

Strategy #1: Come up with your own word

Use this strategy when you read through a sentence and a word just pops into your head. Don't force yourself to try to come up with your own definition when you aren't sure what the word means.

- Use this strategy when the definition pops into your head

If you read a question word and a synonym pops into your head, go ahead and jot it down. It is important that you write down the word because otherwise you may try to talk yourself into an answer choice that "seems to come close". One of the biggest enemies on any standardized test is doubt. Doubt leads to talking yourself into the wrong answer choice, and physically writing down the word gives you the confidence you need when you go through the answer choices.

- Physically write down the definition- don't hold it in your head

After you write down the word, start by crossing out answer choices that are not synonyms for your word. By the time you get down to two choices, you will have a much better idea of what you are looking for.

- Cross out words that don't work

The following drill contains words that you may be able think of a definition for. You should focus on creating good habits with these questions. Even if you see the correct answer, go ahead and write down the word that you were thinking of.

What are good habits?

- Jot down the definition- this will actually save time in the long run
- Use ruling out- physically cross out answer choices that you know are incorrect

Drill #1

1. RAPID:
   (A) ~~exhausted~~
   (B) ~~marvelous~~
   (C) professional
   (D) swift ✓
   quick

2. DAINTY:
   (A) delicate ✓
   (B) long
   (C) ~~surprising~~
   (D) ~~warm~~

3. TIMID:
   (A) ~~alive~~
   (B) damp
   (C) shy ✓
   (D) ~~upset~~

4. CONQUER:
   (A) ~~abandon~~
   (B) defeat ✓
   (C) ~~stun~~
   (D) wander
   Takeover

5. ADMIRE:
   (A) appreciate ✓
   (B) kneel
   (C) ~~nudge~~
   (D) ~~sacrifice~~

(Answers to this drill are found on p. 39)

Strategy #2: Using positive or negative

Sometimes you see a word, and you couldn't define that word, but you have a "gut feeling" that it is either something good or something bad. Maybe you don't know what that word means, but you know you would be mad if someone called you that!

- You have to have a "gut feeling" about a word to use this strategy

To use this strategy, when you get that feeling that a word is either positive or negative, then write in a "+" or a "–" sign next to the word. Then go to your answer choices and rule out anything that is opposite, i.e., positive when your question word is negative or negative when your question word is positive.

- Physically write a "+" or "–" sign after the question word
- Rule out any answer choices that are opposite from your question word

To really make this strategy work for you, you also need to rule out any words that are neutral, or neither positive nor negative. For example, let's say the question word is DISTRESS. Distress is clearly a negative word. So we could rule out a positive answer choice, such as friendly, but we can also rule out a neutral word, such as sleepy. At night, it is good to be sleepy, during the day it is not. Sleepy is not clearly a negative word, so it goes.

- Rule out neutral words

To summarize, here are the basic steps to using this strategy:

1. If you have a gut negative or positive feeling about a word, write a "+" or "–" sign next to the question word
2. Rule out any words that are opposite
3. Also rule out any NEUTRAL words
4. Pick from what is left

Here is an example of a question where you may be able to use the positive/negative strategy:

1. CONDEMN:
   (A) arrive
   (B) blame
   (C) favor
   (D) tint

Let's say that you know that condemn is bad, but you can't think of a definition. We write a – sign next to it and then rule out anything that is positive. That means that choice C can go because it is positive. Now we can also rule out neutral words because we know condemn has to be negative. Arrive and tint are neither positive nor negative, so choices A and D are out. We are left with choice B, which is correct.

On the following drill, write a "+" or "–" sign next to each question word. Then rule out answer choices that are opposite or neutral. Pick from what is left. Even if you aren't sure if the question word is positive or negative, take a guess at it! You may get more right than you would have imagined.

Drill #2

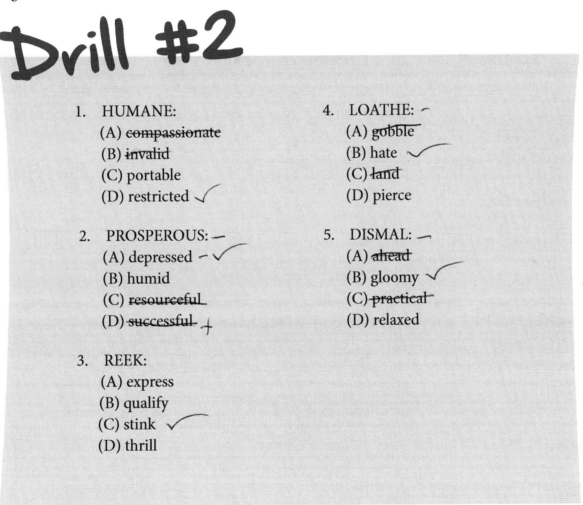

1. HUMANE:
   (A) compassionate
   (B) invalid
   (C) portable
   (D) restricted ✓

2. PROSPEROUS: –
   (A) depressed – ✓
   (B) humid
   (C) resourceful
   (D) successful +

3. REEK:
   (A) express
   (B) qualify
   (C) stink ✓
   (D) thrill

4. LOATHE: –
   (A) gobble
   (B) hate ✓
   (C) land
   (D) pierce

5. DISMAL: –
   (A) ahead
   (B) gloomy ✓
   (C) practical
   (D) relaxed

(Answers to this drill are found on p. 39)

Strategy #3: Use context- Think of where you have heard the word before

Use this strategy when you can't define a word, but you can think of a sentence or phrase where you have heard the word before.

- This strategy only works when you have heard the word before

To apply this strategy, think of a sentence or phrase where you have heard the question word before. Then try plugging the answer choices into your phrase to see which one has the same meaning within that sentence or phrase.

- Think of where you have heard the word before
- Plug question words into that sentence or phrase

Here is an example:

1. ENDORSE:
   (A) drain
   (B) import
   (C) prowl
   (D) support ✓

Let's say that you can't think of a definition for the word "endorse", but you have heard people say that they "endorse a candidate" for political office. Now we plug our answer choices into that phrase and see what would make sense in that context. Would it make sense to "drain a candidate"? Nope. Answer choice A is out. Would it make sense to "import a candidate" or "prowl a candidate"? No and no. Answer choices B and C are out. Finally, would it make sense to say that you "support a candidate"? Absolutely. Answer choice D is correct.

In the following drill, if you have heard the word before, then come up with a sentence or phrase and practice our strategy. If you have not heard the word before, you can't use the strategy of thinking where you have heard the word before! Use another strategy and ruling out to answer the question anyway. You may not answer every question correctly, but remember, nothing ventured, nothing gained.

Keep in mind that all these words would be among the toughest on the test- the whole test will not be this hard! We just want to make sure you have practice for when the going gets tough.

Drill #3

1. WILY:
   (A) cunning ✓
   (B) flattering
   (C) serious
   (D) tough

2. PROPHESY:
   (A) copy
   (B) mystify
   (C) predict ✓
   (D) quiver

3. ABOLISH:
   (A) end ✓
   (B) liberate
   (C) manage
   (D) salute

4. REMARKABLE:
   (A) concerned
   (B) late
   (C) rich
   (D) unusual ✓

5. BRAWNY:
   (A) awake
   (B) coarse
   (C) strong ✓
   (D) tiny

(Answers to this drill are found on p. 39)

Strategy #4: Look for roots or word parts that you know

This strategy works when you recognize that a word looks like another word that you know or when you recognize one of the roots that you have studied in school or in this book.

If you see something familiar in the question word, underline the roots or word parts that you recognize. If you can think of the meaning of the root, then look for answer choices that would go with that meaning. If you can't think of a specific meaning, think of other words that have that root and look for answer choices that are similar in meaning to those other words.

- Underline word parts that you recognize
- Think of the meaning of that word part
- If you can't think of a meaning for that word part, think of other words with that same word part

Here is an example of a question that uses a word with recognizable word parts:

1. EXCLUDE:
    (A) drift
    (B) find
    (C) prohibit
    (D) send

There are two word parts in the word "exclude" that can help us out. First, we have the prefix "ex", which means out (think of the word exit). Secondly, "clu" is a word root that means to shut (think of the word include). Using these word parts, we can see that exclude has something to do with shutting out. Choice C comes closest to this meaning, so it is correct.

For the following drill, try to use word parts to come up with the correct answer choice. If you can't think of what the word root, prefix, or suffix means, then think of other words that have the same root, prefix, or suffix.

Drill #4

1. POSTPONE:
    (A) allow
    (B) delay ✓
    (C) recruit
    (D) tease

2. SUBTERRANEAN:
    (A) faded
    (B) partial
    (C) tragic
    (D) underground ✓

3. CERTIFY:
    (A) confirm ✓
    (B) debate
    (C) ponder
    (D) toss

4. IMPERFECT:
    (A) abandoned
    (B) defective ✓
    (C) separate
    (D) upward

5. BENEFICIAL:
    (A) brisk
    (B) expensive
    (C) helpful ✓
    (D) trim

(Answers to this drill are found on p. 39)

Sentence Completions Strategies

We have several strategies in our toolbox for sentence completion questions.

They include:

- Underlining the key idea
- Look for sentences showing contrast
- Look for sentence showing cause or sequence
- Use our strategies for synonyms when you don't know the meaning of one or more of the answer choices

Strategy #1: Underlining the key idea

Perhaps our most powerful strategy is underlining what the sentence is about.

If you are unsure of what to underline, look for the part of the sentence that if you changed that word or phrase, you would change what you were looking for.

- Look for the part of the sentence that if you changed it, you would change what word or phrase would fit in the blank
- Underline this key word or phrase

After you underline the key word or phrase, try coming up with your own word or phrase that would fit in the blank. This will help you easily rule out answer choices that are not like your word.

- After you underline the key word/phrase, fill in your own word or phrase in the blank

Here is an example:

1. The artist spent his days *painting* the walls in the cave.
2. The scientist spent his days *painting* the walls in the cave.

Do you see how changing just one word changed what we would put in that blank? If the person was an artist, we might expect him to be painting the walls in the cave. If the person was a scientist, however, we would expect him to maybe be studying the walls in the cave or analyzing the walls in the cave.

Below is a drill for you to try. For this drill, you should underline the key word or phrase and then fill in a word that would work for the blank. There are no answer choices for these questions because we just want you to focus on the process of underlining the key word or phrase and filling in your own word at this point.

Drill #5

1. <u>Author</u> Charles Dickens ------ class structure in Victorian London.

   explaines
   Word to fill in the blank?

2. The company received ------ calls after they placed an ad in a <u>widely read</u> publication.

   Many
   Word to fill in the blank?

3. The path seemed to wander in a ----- manner, twisting and turning through the <u>woods</u>.

   unusual
   Word to fill in the blank?

4. The <u>impulsive shopper</u> swooped into the store and filled her cart -------.

   Rapidley
   Word to fill in the blank?

(Answers to this drill are found on p. 40)

Strategy #2: Look for sentences showing contrast

Some sentences show contrast. With these sentences, the end of the sentence changes direction from the beginning of the sentence.

These sentences often use the words "but", "although", "however", "rather", and "even though". If you see any of these words, circle them.

The first step in answering these questions is to underline the key word or phrase. We need to know what we are contrasting with. The next step is to circle the word(s) that shows contrast, such as but, although, however, and even though.

- Underline key word or phrase
- Circle word(s) that show contrast such as but, although, however, rather, and even though

Here is an example:

1. Although the student tried to stay interested, her expression clearly showed that she was -------.
   (A) bored
   (B) jealous
   (C) mysterious
   (D) positive

In this question, we circle the word "although" since it shows contrast. Then we underline the word "interested" since the sentence is about the student staying interested (if we changed that word, we would change what the blank would be). Since we have the word "although" we know that we are looking for a word that contrasts with interested. Since bored is the opposite of interested, choice A is correct.

This type of sentence construction is often used with the questions that have whole phrases as answer choices.

Here is an example:

2. Although Sarah was usually on time for work, when it snowed -------.
   (A) she could not avoid being late for work
   (B) she wore a colorful scarf and earmuffs to work
   (C) she was cold all day long
   (D) she booked a vacation in the tropics

The trick to this question is to pay close attention to the beginning of the sentence. The beginning of the sentence talks about how Sarah is usually on time for work. It also has the word "although" so we know that we are looking for something that is the opposite of being on time for work. Only choice A contrasts with being on time for work, so it is the correct answer. For this question it would be really easy to focus on the fact that it is snowing. If we are just paying attention to the snow, then choices B, C, and D would be possibilities. To avoid falling for this trap, go back to the basics. Underline the key word or phrase in the beginning of the sentence and stick to that.

In the following drill, you should circle the word showing contrast, underline the key word/phrase, and choose an answer choice that contrasts with your key word or phrase.

1. His teachers always <u>predicted</u> that Sam would not be successful as an adult <u>but</u> he founded a company that -------.
   (A) failed
   (B) limped
   (C) managed
   (D) thrived ✓

2. Although Kara was often tardy, on the day of her birthday she was always -------.
   (A) active ✓
   (B) happy
   (C) prompt
   (D) tense

3. Critics <u>said</u> that the musician's new album would be a flop, <u>but</u> album sales were instead------.
   (A) definite
   (B) limited
   (C) slender
   (D) strong ✓

Drill #6 (cont.)

4. Even though there was a big crowd at the event, it was surprisingly --------.
   (A) calm ✓
   (B) impolite
   (C) rowdy
   (D) tedious

5. People often think of China as having a large population, however, there are several regions of China that have ----- inhabitants.
   (A) beloved
   (B) few
   (C) regular ✓
   (D) typical

6. Although Ansel Adams was unsuccessful as a student, he later --------.
   (A) became a very well-known photographer ✓
   (B) ran a business that failed
   (C) produced photographs of natural scenes
   (D) travelled a lot

7. In contrast to many factories where one worker created an entire product from beginning to end, Henry Ford's factories -------.
   (A) made a huge profit
   (B) used many workers to create a single product ✓
   (C) produced cars
   (D) were moved to another country

(Answers to this drill are found on p. 40)

Strategy #3: Look for sentences showing cause or sequence

Many sentences in the sentence completions section use the cause or sequence relationship. In these sentences, one thing leads to another. Sometimes one directly causes the other, but sometimes one just happens to come after the other.

- Look for sentences where one thing leads to another
- Think about what the effect of the given action would be

Sometimes you will see the words "because", "when", or "after" in these sentences, but there is often no one particular word that indicates cause.

- If you see the words "because", "when", "after", or other words showing sequence, you usually have a sentence showing cause or sequence

Here is an example:

1. Years of floods and fires left the former resort ------.
   (A) busy
   (B) effective
   (C) patriotic
   (D) wrecked ✓

To answer this question, we have to ask ourselves what years of floods and fires would lead to. While you could say that the resort would be left busy because they had lot of clean up work to do, the more direct answer would be that it was left wrecked. Choice D is the correct answer.

Here is a drill for you to try.

Drill #7

1. After she finished all of her college applications, Abby went out to dinner to ------.
   (A) celebrate ✓
   (B) host
   (C) sleep
   (D) write

2. It is clear that schoolwork is a priority for Lee because he ------- frequently.
   (A) cleans
   (B) enchants
   (C) meddles
   (D) studies ✓

3. When George entered a room where he didn't know anyone, he felt rather-------.
   (A) backward
   (B) defensive
   (C) nervous ✓
   (D) quaint

4. The increase in the number of students forced the school district to consider ----- schools.
   (A) accomplishing
   (B) adding ✓
   (C) limiting
   (D) painting

5. The damage caused by the tornado was ------.
   (A) camouflaged
   (B) efficient
   (C) musty
   (D) tragic ✓

6. When part of their habitat was destroyed, the lynx cats in the area -------.
   (A) grew lighter coats
   (B) were greatly reduced in ✓ number
   (C) became more numerous
   (D) were renamed by scientists

7. Since the dance team won a large cash prize, they ------.
   (A) changed their performance
   (B) came up with a new name
   (C) could afford to travel to another competition ✓
   (D) dissolved the team

(Answers to this drill are found on p. 40)

Strategy #4: Use our strategies for synonyms when you don't know the meaning of one or more of the answer choices

Sometimes you know what kind of word you are looking for, but the problem is that you don't know the meaning of some of the answer choices. If this is the case, ask yourself:

- Am I looking for a positive or negative word?
- Do any of the answer choices have roots or prefixes that I can use?
- Have I heard any of the answer choices used in a sentence or phrase before?

In the following drill, practice using our strategies of looking for a positive or a negative word, looking for roots or word parts that you know, or thinking of where you have heard an answer choice before. You may not be certain of the answer choice that you choose, but by using ruling out you are more likely to answer questions correctly.

Drill #8

1. The majestic mountain views often leave visitors feeling ------.
   (A) awe ✓
   (B) bored
   (C) loud
   (D) tired

2. Since the mall was nicely redone and more parking was added, the restaurant business there has --------.
   (A) crumbled
   (B) flapped
   (C) thrived ✓
   (D) vanished

3. Mother Teresa showed her ------ by helping people who lived in poverty.
   (A) accuracy
   (B) compassion ✓
   (C) irritation
   (D) technique

4. The school focuses on ------ classes such as pottery, drawing, and sculpture.
   (A) artistic ✓
   (B) history
   (C) literature
   (D) science

5. The sides of the shape are not all the same size, rather they are ------.
   (A) adjoining
   (B) buckled
   (C) familiar
   (D) irregular ✓

6. If a piece of paper is no longer usable it should be -------.
   (A) bought
   (B) discarded ✓
   (C) mysterious
   (D) treasured

7. When the runner won the marathon, the local press praised her ------- performance.
   (A) dry
   (B) minor
   (C) superlative ✓
   (D) wild

Now you have the skills that you need to do well on the Verbal Reasoning section of the ISEE! An important part of improving your verbal reasoning score is also studying vocabulary. Be sure to spend time with the following vocabulary section.

Answers to Synonyms Drills

Drill #1

1. D
2. A
3. C
4. B
5. A

Drill #2

1. A
2. D
3. C
4. B
5. B

Drill #3

1. A
2. C
3. A
4. D
5. C

Drill #4

1. B
2. D
3. A
4. B
5. C

Answers to Sentence Completion Drills

Drill #5

1. Underline "author", fill in a word like "describes"
2. Underline "widely read", fill in a word like "many"
3. Underline "twisting and turning", fill in a word like "indirect"
4. Underline "impulsive", fill in a word like "quickly"

Drill #6

1. D
2. C
3. D
4. A
5. B
6. A
7. B

Drill #7

1. A
2. D
3. C
4. B
5. D
6. B
7. C

Drill #8

1. A
2. C
3. B
4. A
5. D
6. B
7. C

Vocabulary Review

A key component of improving your verbal score is increasing your vocabulary. Following are ten lessons that will help you do just that.

Each lesson has twenty new words for you to learn. There are good words, there are bad words, and there are even words with roots. Exciting, eh?

After you learn the words, complete the activities for each lesson. The best way to learn new words is to think of them in categories and to evaluate how the words relate to one another. The activities will help you do this.

The activities also give you practice with synonyms and sentence completions. You will be working on strategy while you are learning new words- think of it as a two for one! Be aware that the synonym and sentence completion questions may have a different form of the word than is given in the word list. This is by design so that you get used to looking for words that are similar to the words that you have learned.

If there are words that you have trouble remembering as you work through the lessons, go ahead and make flashcards for them. Continue to review these flashcards until the words stick. There may also be words that you run across in the analogies or synonyms practice that you do not know the meaning of. Make flashcards for these words as well.

After each lesson are the answers. Be sure to check your work.

Now, on to the lessons!

Lesson One

Words to Learn

Below are the twenty words used in Lesson One; refer back to this list as needed as you move through the lesson.

Disobey: defy (to break or not follow the rules)
Prosper: succeed
Frank: honest (really, really honest)
Coy: sly (holding back)
Bustle: hurry

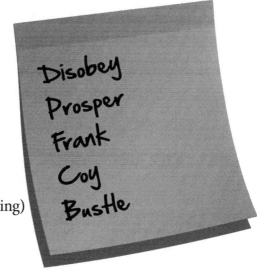

Dismal: gloomy
Prolong: lengthen (make longer)
Counterfeit: fake (or to make a fake copy of something)
Brisk: fast-moving
Disdain: a lack of respect or to consider unworthy

Hasty: rushed
Adorn: decorate
Bluff: deceive
Abrupt: sudden
Cunning: tricky

Rash: reckless (done without thought)
Decoy: a copy or fake
Discourage: to encourage a person NOT to do something
Blunt: direct (honest, even when it isn't nice)
Wily: clever

Word List Practice

Use the words from the Lesson One list to answer the following questions.

1. If you ask a person how your hair looks and you want an honest answer, then you would ask a person to be:
   a. Frank
   b. Blunt

2. If you ask a person if your outfit looks good and you just want them to tell you yes, you might hope that when they answer they will be:
   a. Coy

3. If you are looking for a business partner, you would NOT want someone who is:
   a. Disobidient
   b. Disdain

4. In spy movies, the bad guys often use a decoy to mislead the good guys. What does it mean to use a decoy in this case?

   to act as someone they're not.

5. If I tell you that the money was counterfeit, what do I mean?

   Fake

6. If a wreathe on the door looks very plain, I might want someone to ___adorn___ it with bows and ribbons.

7. What five words in our list relate to being in a hurry?
   a. Hasty
   b. Rash
   c. Bustle
   d. Brisk
   e. abrupt

8. If you are in a hurry, you might walk at a ___Brisk___ pace.

9. If you are running late for a class, you would ___Bustle___ to class.

10. Would you want someone to bluff when talking with you? Why or why not?

Roots Practice

11. We have four words in our list with the "dis" root. What are they?
    a. Disobey
    b. Dismay
    c. Discourage
    d. Disdain

12. Looking at the words above with the "dis" prefix, do you think the "dis" root has a positive or negative meaning? negative NEGATIVE

13. We have two words in our list with the "pro" prefix. What are they?
    a. prolong
    b. prosper

14. Looking at the words in our list with the "pro" prefix, do you think the "pro" prefix is generally positive or negative? positive

Synonyms Practice

1. FRANK:
   (A) blunt ✓
   (B) easy
   (C) famous
   (D) ridiculous

2. PROSPER:
   (A) discourage
   (B) imagine
   (C) puzzle
   (D) succeed ✓

3. RASH:
   (A) adorned
   (B) hasty ✓
   (C) peaceful
   (D) settled

4. DISMAL:
   (A) abrupt
   (B) firm
   (C) gloomy ✓
   (D) ragged

5. COUNTERFEIT:
   (A) fake ✓
   (B) jealous
   (C) rehearsed
   (D) thrilling

Sentence Completions Practice

1. During a poker game, a player may ------- so that the other players do not know how good her hand is.
   (A) bluff ✓
   (B) disobey
   (C) govern
   (D) narrate

2. The politician was purposefully -------- so that his constituents would not know his involvement in a tax scandal.
   (A) brisk
   (B) coy ✓
   (C) overhead
   (D) thankful

3. Author John Kennedy Toole was treated with ------- by publishers during his life, but was eventually given the Pulitzer Prize for Fiction after his death.
   (A) cunning
   (B) disdain ✓
   (C) quality
   (D) respect

4. New York City is often described as an active place full of people who are ------- to their next appointments.
   (A) bustling ✓
   (B) entertaining
   (C) prolonging
   (D) yelping

5. Duck hunters often use a ------ so that other ducks would think it was safe to swim in the pond.
   (A) absence
   (B) barge
   (C) cushion
   (D) decoy ✓

6. In a popular children's cartoon, when the coyote tricks the roadrunner into falling off a cliff, the coyote is being quite -------.
   (A) admirable
   (B) humble
   (C) rusty
   (D) wily ✓

Lesson One Answers

Word List Practice

1. a. blunt ✓
   b. frank ✓
2. a. coy ✓
3. a. cunning
   b. wily
4. The bad guys use a decoy, or someone who looks just like them, so
   that the good guys will follow the ✓
   decoy instead of the real bad guys.
5. The money looked real... but it ✓
   wasn't actually real money.
6. adorn ✓
7. a. abrupt ✓
   b. rash ✓
   c. brisk ✓
   d. bustle ✓
   e. hasty ✓
8. brisk ✓
9. bustle ✓
10. No. You would want the truth.

Roots Practice

11. a. disobey ✓
    b. discourage ✓
    c. disdain ✓
    d. dismal ✓
12. negative- in general it means to do
    the opposite of (as in disobey and
    discourage) or to just generally be ✓
    bad or negative (as in disdain or
    dismal)

13. a. prosper
    b. prolong
14. positive

Synonyms Practice

1. A ✓
2. D ✓
3. B ✓
4. C ✓
5. A ✓

Sentence Completions

1. A ✓
2. B ✓
3. B ✓
4. A ✓
5. D ✓
6. D ✓

Lesson Two

Words to Learn

Below are the twenty words used in Lesson Two; refer back to this list as needed as you move through the lesson.

Chasm: gorge (a hole or break that seems bottomless)
Primary: main (most important)
Gaunt: skinny (very, very skinny)
Relent: surrender (to give in)
Adjacent: bordering (next to)

Nimble: quick
Crest: top
Ailing: sick
Recede: decrease (go back)
Adjoining: touching

Remorse: guilt
Agile: athletic (quick)
Crevice: crack (narrow opening)
Remnant: leftover
Lanky: tall and thin

Retort: reply
Limber: flexible
Minor: unimportant
Recollection: memory
Adhesive: sticking

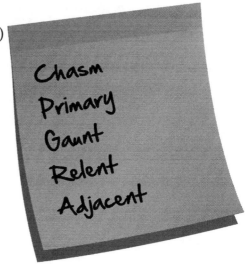

Chasm
Primary
Gaunt
Relent
Adjacent

Word List Practice

Use the words from the Lesson Two list to answer the following questions.

1. What words might you use to describe a gymnast?
   a. Gaunt
   b. Agile
   c. Limber

2. What is the difference between gaunt and lanky?

   Gaunt is extreamly skinny and lanky is tion and thin

3. If someone was ailing, would they more likely be described as gaunt or lanky?

   gaunt

4. What is bigger, a chasm or a crevice?

   chasm

5. What do we call the top of a wave?

   crest

6. If you are driving to an event, would the location be a primary concern or a minor concern?

   Primary

7. If you are not really hungry, would the food being served be a primary concern or a minor concern?

   minor

Roots Practice

1. There are six words in our lesson that have "re" as a prefix. What are they?
   a. *reamorse*
   b. *remnant*
   c. *relent*
   d. *retort*
   e. *recollection*
   f. *recede*

2. From these words, what do you think "re" means as a prefix?

   redo

3. If a hairline is receding, what does that mean?

   goes back

4. What is going back in the word recollection?

   receda

5. If you feel remorse, what would you want to do?

   go back and tell the truth

6. If you ask your mother for a game that she already said no to, would you want her to relent or retort?

   relent

7. Three words in our unit have the prefix "ad". What are they?
   a. *adjoining*
   b. *adhesive*
   c. *adjacent*

8. From these words, what do you think the prefix "ad" means?

   adding on

9. If adhesive means sticking and cohesive means sticking together closely, what do you think the "hes" root means?

to stick to

Synonyms Practice

1. LIMBER:
   (A) ailing
   (B) flexible ✓
   (C) irregular
   (D) noble

2. ADJACENT:
   (A) adjoining ✓
   (B) old-fashioned
   (C) plump
   (D) quick

3. CHASM:
   (A) dozen
   (B) fact
   (C) gorge ✓
   (D) retort

4. PRIMARY:
   (A) dried
   (B) important ✓
   (C) nimble
   (D) special

5. CREST:
   (A) human
   (B) myth
   (C) remnant
   (D) top ✓

Sentence Completion Practice

1. After Hurricane Sandy caused a flood in lower Manhattan, the water slowly ------- and only then could clean up of the area begin.
   (A) answered
   (B) doubled
   (C) pondered
   (D) receded ✓

2. Marie Antoinette, who was queen of France from 1774 to 1792, did not appear ------- when she was told that French citizens were starving, so history has treated her cruelly.
   (A) adhesive
   (B) gaunt
   (C) remorseful
   (D) tidy

3. With its long neck, thin body, and skinny legs, the African giraffe could be described as --------.
   (A) courteous
   (B) lanky
   (C) minor
   (D) neutral

4. Luray Caverns, in Virginia, was discovered when a group of local men slid into a ------- and the land opened up to reveal a network of hidden caves.
   (A) crevice
   (B) filter
   (C) movement
   (D) recollection

5. Although its leaders had sworn to never surrender, on April 9, 1865, the Confederate Army ------- and the American Civil War ended.
   (A) focused
   (B) identified
   (C) relented
   (D) tempted

6. Arthur Ashe showed that he was one of the most ------- tennis players of his generation when he lunged for the ball and returned a nearly impossible dropshot.
   (A) agile
   (B) common
   (C) limited
   (D) thrifty

Lesson Two Answers

Word List Practice

1. a. agile
   b. nimble
   c. limber
2. Lanky could describe a person who is tall and skinny, but healthy. Gaunt implies that a person is unhealthily skinny.
3. Gaunt
4. Chasm
5. Crest
6. Primary
7. Minor

Roots Practice

1. a. recollection
   b. remnant
   c. relent
   d. retort
   e. recede
   f. remorse
2. back or again
3. it is going back
4. memory
5. go back and do things differently
6. relent
7. a. adhesive
   b. adjoining
   c. adjacent
8. to or toward
9. to stick

Synonyms Practice

1. B
2. A
3. C
4. B
5. D

Sentence Completions

1. D
2. C
3. B
4. A
5. C
6. A

Lesson Three

Words to Learn

Below are the twenty words used in Lesson Three; refer back to this list as needed as you move through the lesson.

Subdue: calm (to make less active)
Preface: introduction
Definite: certain
Courteous: polite
Competent: capable (able to do a job)

Subside: decrease
Industrious: hard-working
Prevail: win
Gruff: rude
Cordial: friendly

Submarine: underwater vehicle
Absolute: unquestionable
Labor: work
Civilized: well-mannered
Idle: inactive

Submerge: immerse (put completely underwater)
Precede: come before
Provisional: conditional (depending upon something else)
Persist: continue (not give up)
Toil: hard work

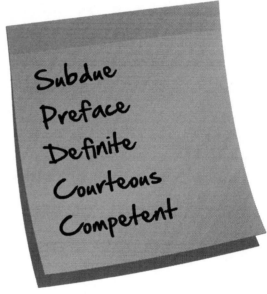

Subdue
Preface
Definite
Courteous
Competent

Word List Practice

1. What five words from the word list could describe a good employee?

   a.

   b.

   c.

   d.

   e.

2. You wouldn't want to work with the people described by these two words:

   a.

   b.

3. These two words both describe work:

   a.

   b.

4. When people say, "Persistence is the key to success", what do they mean?

5. Which two words would you use if you were completely certain that something would happen?

   a.

   b.

6. What word would you use if you weren't completely sure that something would happen?

Roots Practice

1. There are four words in this lesson that have the root "sub". What are they?

   a.

   b.

   c.

   d.

2. From the meaning of these words, what you think the root "sub" means?

3. There are three words that have the root "pre" in them on our list. What are they?

   a.

   b.

   c.

4. The "pre" root means before. How does "prevail" relate to this meaning?

Synonyms Practice

1. CIVILIZED:
   (A) absolute
   (B) polite
   (C) successful
   (D) waiting

2. TOIL:
   (A) labor
   (B) nag
   (C) submerge
   (D) turn

3. GRUFF:
   (A) anxious
   (B) competent
   (C) rude
   (D) spectacular

4. PREFACE:
   (A) ditch
   (B) introduction
   (C) laughter
   (D) submarine

5. DEFINITE:
   (A) certain
   (B) foreign
   (C) subdued
   (D) tight

Sentence Completion Practice

1. Thomas Edison was known for being ------, applying for over 1,000 patents in his lifetime.
   (A) courteous
   (B) industrious
   (C) lonesome
   (D) scowling

2. Although she was accepted into the college, her acceptance was ------- and the college wanted to see that her grades improved in the final semester.
   (A) binding
   (B) dainty
   (C) idle
   (D) provisional

3. Mary Todd Lincoln was not known for being -------, rather she was often viewed as being rude and unfriendly to guests.
   (A) cordial
   (B) ideal
   (C) persistent
   (D) triumphant

4. Many scientists believe that a meteor hitting Earth ------- the extinction of the dinosaurs and that the dinosaurs died off shortly after a meteor struck the Yucatan Peninsula in Mexico.
   (A) advertised
   (B) debated
   (C) preceded
   (D) subsided

5. Without a -------, a book about a complex historical event can be hard to comprehend since it is often necessary to understand the background that led up to the event.
   (A) absence
   (B) cushion
   (C) preface
   (D) value

6. The United States men's hockey team stunned the world when they ------- over the much more successful Russian team in the 1980 Olympic Games in Lake Placid.
   (A) believed
   (B) prevailed
   (C) ran
   (D) whisked

Lesson Three Answers

Word List Practice

1. a. courteous
   b. competent
   c. industrious
   d. cordial
   e. civilized
2. a. gruff
   b. idle
3. a. toil
   b. labor
4. You have to persist, or stick with work even when it is hard, in order to succeed.
5. a. definite
   b. absolute
6. provisional

Roots Practice

1. a. subdue
   b. subside
   c. submarine
   d. submerge
2. under
3. a. preface
   b. prevail
   c. precede
4. The "pre" part of the word means before, and the "vail" part of the word comes from "valere", which is Latin for to be strong. So if you prevail, you are strong first, or defeat the other person.

Synonyms Practice

1. B
2. A
3. C
4. B
5. A

Sentence Completions

1. B
2. D
3. A
4. C
5. C
6. B

Lesson Four

Words to Learn

Below are the twenty words used in Lesson Four; refer back to this list as needed as you move through the lesson.

Descend: lower (to go down)
Novice: beginner
Accustomed: used to
Despair: hopelessness
Peculiar: unusual

Decline: drop
Novel: new
Conventional: ordinary
Innovate: invent (to make new)
Destruction: ruin

Wretched: miserable
Distinct: different
Commence: begin
Unique: strange (one of a kind)
Defy: resist

Alien: unfamiliar
Detour: bypass (not a direct path)
Singular: unmatched (one of a kind)
Customary: common
Vile: horrible

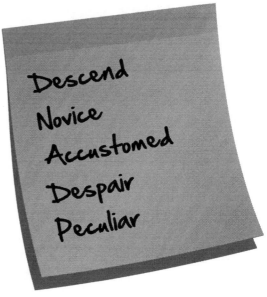

Descend
Novice
Accustomed
Despair
Peculiar

Word List Practice

1. These three words could all be used to describe something that is one of a kind:
   a.
   b.
   c.

2. These two words could describe something that is just plain weird, but not necessarily one of a kind:
   a.
   b.

3. If you are accustomed to eating breakfast before school, what does that mean?

4. If it is customary to tip a waiter 15% in a restaurant, what does that mean?

5. In a grocery store, you may see produce labeled either "organic" or "conventional". Why is food labeled "conventional" if it is not organic?

6. What two words would describe the wicked stepmother in Cinderella?
   a.
   b.

7. At a graduation, there is often a commencement speech. Given that commence means to begin, why do they call a speech at a graduation a commencement speech?

Roots Practice

1. There are three words in our list that have the "nov" root. What are they?

   a.

   b.

   c.

2. From the meanings of these words, what do you think the meaning of the root "nov" is?

3. There are six words in our list with the prefix "de". What are they?

   a.

   b.

   c.

   d.

   e.

   f.

4. From these words, do you think that words that begin with "de" are generally positive or negative?

Synonyms Practice

1. SINGULAR:
   (A) advanced
   (B) determined
   (C) rusty
   (D) unique

2. CONVENTIONAL:
   (A) easy
   (B) novel
   (C) ordinary
   (D) remarkable

3. VILE:
   (A) abrupt
   (B) efficient
   (C) rare
   (D) wretched

4. DISTINCT:
   (A) different
   (B) innovative
   (C) polished
   (D) sneaky

5 DESPAIR:
   (A) alien
   (B) misery
   (C) racket
   (D) undertaking

Sentence Completions Practice

1. When Howard Carter ------- into King Tut's underground tomb, he immediately knew he that he had made an important discovery.
   (A) commenced
   (B) descended
   (C) informed
   (D) pondered

2. It is dangerous for -------- to attempt to climb Mt. Everest due to their lack of experience.
   (A) declines
   (B) experiments
   (C) novices
   (D) somebody

3. Edgar Allan Poe's ------- appearance matched the imaginative and fanciful stories that he wrote.
   (A) accustomed
   (B) destructive
   (C) peculiar
   (D) truthful

4. When there is construction on a road, often a ------- must be set up.
   (A) detour
   (B) hotel
   (C) sidewalk
   (D) truck

5. In the Japanese culture, it is ------- to bow when you meet a person.
   (A) beautiful
   (B) customary
   (C) hazardous
   (D) musical

6. The American colonists ------ the British Parliament when the Stamp Act was passed in 1765, which in part led to the American Revolution.
   (A) defied
   (B) envied
   (C) knew
   (D) signaled

Lesson Four Answers

Word List Practice

1. a. unique
   b. singular
   c. distinct
2. a. peculiar
   b. alien
3. It means that you are used to eating breakfast before school.
4. It means that you don't absolutely have to tip 15%, but that is what is expected, or normal.
5. Most food is not raised organically, so it is considered conventional if common agricultural practices are used to grow the food.
6. a. vile
   b. wretched
7. After a graduation, students are headed off to begin a new life, so the commencement speech gives advice on this new beginning.

Roots Practice

1. a. innovate
   b. novel
   c. novice
2. new
3. a. descend
   b. decline
   c. despair
   d. detour
   e. destruction
   f. defy
4. negative

Synonyms

1. D
2. C
3. D
4. A
5. B

Sentence Completions

1. B
2. C
3. C
4. A
5. B
6. A

Lesson Five

Words to Learn

Below are the twenty words used in Lesson Five; refer back to this list as needed as you move through the lesson.

Absurd: ridiculous
Enforce: implement (to make people follow a law)
Quarantine: isolation (to prevent disease)
Dawn: sunrise
Punctual: prompt (on time)

Absent: missing
Fortify: strengthen
Limited: restricted
Tardy: late
Remote: distant

Seldom: rarely (not often)
Abolish: end (do away with)
Fortitude: strength
Dusk: sunset
Banish: exile (to kick someone out)

Abnormal: weird
Era: a set period of time (usually in years)
Forge: form (to make)
Eventual: later (will happen in the future)
Infinite: limitless

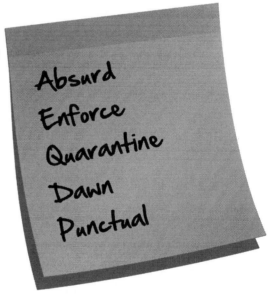

Absurd
Enforce
Quarantine
Dawn
Punctual

Word List Practice

1. If you never wanted to see someone again, what would you do to him or her?

2. If you simply didn't want to catch a person's illness, what would you do to him or her?

3. If you didn't want to see anyone else, what kind of place would you want to live in?

4. We have a word in our list that means the opposite of limited. What is that word?

5. If you are a very punctual person, what kind of person would annoy you?

6. What do people mean when they say that something was "an end of an era"?

7. If you are a rock star, are you more likely to get out of bed at dawn or at dusk?

8. What word do we use to describe something that does not happen very often?

9. What word do we use to describe something that will happen in the future?

Roots Practice

1. What four words in our lesson have the prefix "ab-"?

   a.

   b.

   c.

   d.

2. From these words, what do you think the meaning of the "ab-" prefix is?

3. What four words in this lesson have the forc/forg/fort root? (Even though the spelling of this root may vary, the different forms still have the same meaning.)

   a.

   b.

   c.

   d.

4. From these words, what do you think the forc/forg/fort root means?

Synonyms Practice

1. ABSURD:
   (A) favorable
   (B) independent
   (C) ridiculous
   (D) seldom

2. FORTIFY:
   (A) abolish
   (B) grieve
   (C) promote
   (D) strengthen

3. INFINITE:
   (A) eventual
   (B) limitless
   (C) painful
   (D) superior

4. DAWN:
   (A) era
   (B) fortitude
   (C) identity
   (D) sunrise

5. BANISH:
   (A) exile
   (B) forge
   (C) lecture
   (D) pour

Sentence Completion Practice

1. An outbreak of the influenza during World War I led to the ------ of many soldiers so that others would not be infected.
   (A) fighting
   (B) insult
   (C) quarantine
   (D) vocation

2. Seatbelt laws can be tough to ------ since it can be difficult for officers to see if a person is wearing a seatbelt in a car that is moving quickly.
   (A) absent
   (B) enforce
   (C) remove
   (D) weigh

3. In the novel Robinson Crusoe, a sailor is shipwrecked on a ------ island in the middle of the Pacific Ocean.
   (A) counterfeit
   (B) limited
   (C) nimble
   (D) remote

4. It is not ------ in some cultures for children to be named after their grandparents, in fact, it happens frequently.
   (A) abnormal
   (B) punctual
   (C) tardy
   (D) vicious

5. Many birdwatchers wait anxiously for the sun to set since many birds come out to hunt at -------.
   (A) basins
   (B) dusk
   (C) inventions
   (D) rivers

Lesson Five Answers

Word List Practice

1. banish him or her
2. quarantine him or her
3. a remote place
4. infinite
5. a frequently tardy person
6. An era is a time period that is marked by having characteristics that are different from other time periods. Often a single event marks the beginning of a new era. For example, the 1920's in America were known for many people making money very quickly, but when the stock market crashed in 1929, it was the end of that era.
7. dusk
8. seldom
9. eventual

Roots Practice

1. a. absurd
   b. abnormal
   c. abolish
   d. absent
2. away or off
3. a. enforce
   b. forge
   c. fortify
   d. fortitude
4. strength

Synonyms Practice

1. C
2. D
3. B
4. D
5. A

Sentence Completions

1. C
2. B
3. D
4. A
5. B

Lesson Six

Words to Learn

Below are the twenty words used in Lesson Six; refer back to this list as needed as you move through the lesson.

Desolate: deserted
Capable: skilled (able to do something)
Flimsy: weak
Adapt: change
Hardy: strong

Preventable: avoidable (can be stopped before it happens)
Enrage: anger
Solitary: alone
Portable: easily moved
Brittle: fragile (easily broken)

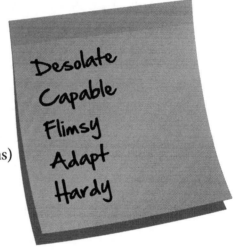

Isolate: separate
Disable: damage
Mend: repair
Mangled: damaged
Alter: change

Sole: only
Suitable: appropriate
Amend: improve
Mighty: powerful
Fury: rage

Word List Practice

1. What four words in our list could describe making a change?

   a.

   b.

   c.

   d.

2. What words describe someone or something that is big and strong?

   a.

   b.

3. What words would describe something that is definitely NOT big and strong?

   a.

   b.

   c.

4. What words go with getting really, really mad?

   a.

   b.

Roots Practice

1. There are four words in our list that have the "sol" root. What are they?

   a.

   b.

   c.

   d.

2. From these words, what do you think that the root "sol" means?

3. The suffix "-able" means, well, able to do something. Given that the word disable means to damage, do you think that the "dis" root is positive or negative? How does the root "able" relate to the meaning of disable?

4. If capable means that you can do something, what do you think incapable means?

5. If portable means that something can be carried or moved, what do you think the "port" root means?

6. Would it be suitable to wear a sweater on a hot summer day?

7. When doctors talk about "preventable diseases", what do they mean?

Synonym Practice

1. HARDY:
   (A) capable
   (B) false
   (C) strong
   (D) treasured

2. DESOLATE:
   (A) deserted
   (B) gracious
   (C) lame
   (D) flimsy

3. BRITTLE:
   (A) adaptable
   (B) fragile
   (C) general
   (D) minor

4. ENRAGE:
   (A) anger
   (B) disable
   (C) nestle
   (D) wedge

5. MANGLED:
   (A) beige
   (B) creaky
   (C) damaged
   (D) suitable

Sentence Completion Practice:

1. The writers of the Constitution included ways to ------- the document so that changes could be made as the United States grew.
   (A) amend
   (B) ditch
   (C) host
   (D) mystify

2. When Jonas Salk invented the vaccine for polio, it became a ------ disease instead of a disabling scourge.
   (A) known
   (B) mighty
   (C) preventable
   (D) sole

3. Due to their -------- location, the Galapagos Islands became a refuge for many bird species because the birds were separated from the predators that made them extinct in more populated areas.
   (A) binding
   (B) isolated
   (C) portable
   (D) subtle

4. Henry David Thoreau moved to the woods by himself because he felt that a ------- life would allow him to grow as an individual.
   (A) altered
   (B) muffled
   (C) rapid
   (D) solitary

5. Although the tear in the painting seemed significant, the curators at the Smithsonian museum were able to ------ the canvas.
   (A) boost
   (B) mend
   (C) repeat
   (D) test

6. In Greek mythology, a group of angry goddesses would seek revenge in a show of -------.
   (A) fury
   (B) leisure
   (C) merit
   (D) respect

Lesson Six Answers

Word List Practice

1. a. amend
   b. adapt
   c. alter
   d. mend
2. a. hardy
   b. mighty
3. a. brittle
   b. flimsy
   c. mangled
4. a. fury
   b. enrage

Roots Practice

1. a. desolate
   b. isolate
   c. sole
   d. solitary
2. alone
3. negative, if something is damaged then it is not able to do something
4. not able to do something
5. to carry
6. no
7. "Preventable diseases" are those that can be stopped before people are infected. For example, we have a vaccine for polio, so that is now a preventable disease.

Synonyms Practice

1. C
2. A
3. B
4. A
5. C

Sentence Completion Practice

1. A
2. C
3. B
4. D
5. B
6. A

Lesson Seven

Words to Learn

Below are the twenty words used in Lesson Seven; refer back to this list as needed as you move through the lesson.

Exhaust: tire (to wear out or use up)
Vivid: bright or memorable
Alliance: partnership
Comrade: friend
Sullen: grumpy

Expedition: trip (usually a big journey)
Vista: view
Accompany: join (to go with someone else)
Unruly: uncontrollable (badly behaved)
Ease: lessen (make easier)

Export: send (to another country)
Allegiance: loyalty
Insolent: disrespectful
Exhibit: show (in public)
Associate: partner

Extract: remove
Quench: satisfy
Amiable: friendly
Evident: clear
Soothe: calm

Word List Practice

1. What are two words that you could call a friend or partner?

   a.

   b.

2. If two people are friends, what might they form?

3. If they do form an alliance, what might they pledge to the alliance?

4. If someone was a friend, you might ask him or her to do what on a trip?

5. What word would describe a person that you would like to be friends with?

6. What three words would describe someone that you would NOT want to be friends with?

   a.

   b.

   c.

7. What three words describe making something better?

   a.

   b.

   c.

Roots Practice

1. There are five words in our list that have the "ex-" prefix. What are they?
   a.
   b.
   c.
   d.
   e.

2. Based on these words, what do you think the "ex-" prefix means?

3. If you are exhausted, what are you out of?

4. In lesson six, we learned that "port" means to carry. What does export literally mean?

5. Extract means to remove, or pull out. What do you think the "tract" root means?

6. We have three words with the vid/vis root. What are they?
   a.
   b.
   c.

7. Based on these words, what does the vid/vis root mean?

Synonyms Practice

1. COMRADE:
   (A) associate
   (B) frost
   (C) position
   (D) speck

2. AMIABLE:
   (A) exhausted
   (B) friendly
   (C) secure
   (D) thrifty

3. EASE:
   (A) accompany
   (B) meet
   (C) object
   (D) soothe

4. INSOLENT:
   (A) disrespectful
   (B) noisy
   (C) positive
   (D) vivid

5. QUENCH:
   (A) export
   (B) jeer
   (C) satisfy
   (D) reply

Sentence Completion Practice

1. During World War II, France's ------ with Great Britain allowed those two countries to band together and drive back German troops.
   (A) alliance
   (B) exhibit
   (C) opinion
   (D) tension

2. The hiking trails in the Rocky Mountain National Park provide for stunning------ of the surrounding mountains.
   (A) allegiances
   (B) departures
   (C) movements
   (D) vistas

3. Although she grew up to be a wildly successful author, Louisa May Alcott was known as an ------- child.
   (A) evident
   (B) genuine
   (C) magnificent
   (D) unruly

4. Robert Peary is famous for his ------- to the North Pole in 1909.
   (A) capsule
   (B) expedition
   (C) imagination
   (D) position

5. When a tooth becomes infected, it often must be --------.
   (A) extracted
   (B) offered
   (C) rushed
   (D) suspected

6. The filmmaker was known for his gloomy and ------- main characters.
   (A) cheerful
   (B) detailed
   (C) sullen
   (D) tremendous

Lesson Seven Answers

Word List Practice

1. a. comrade
   b. associate
2. an alliance
3. allegiance
4. accompany you
5. amiable
6. a. unruly
   b. sullen
   c. insolent
7. a. quench
   b. ease
   c. soothe

Roots Practice

1. a. exhaust
   b. exhibit
   c. expedition
   d. export
   e. extract
2. out
3. energy
4. to carry out
5. to pull
6. a. evident
   b. vivid
   c. vista
7. to see

Synonym Practice

1. A
2. B
3. D
4. A
5. C

Sentence Completion Practice

1. A
2. D
3. D
4. B
5. A
6. C

Lesson Eight

Words to Learn

Below are the twenty words used in Lesson Eight; refer back to this list as needed as you move through the lesson.

Compel: force (make someone do something)
Gratitude: appreciation
Astound: astonish (greatly surprise)
Colossal: huge
Scant: small (usually an amount)

Expel: eject (force out)
Baffle: confuse
Stun: shock
Magnify: increase
Immense: enormous

Repel: force away
Gracious: polite
Meager: small
Dainty: delicate
Bewilder: confuse

Propel: push
Astonishment: amazement
Fluster: upset
Majesty: greatness
Slight: insignificant

Compel
Gratitude
Astound
Colossal
Scant

Word List Practice

1. If you saw flying monkeys, what five words relate to how you would feel?
   a.
   b.
   c.
   d.
   e.

2. If you lost your keys, what word relates to how you would feel?

3. What words relate to a large size or greatness?
   a.
   b.
   c.
   d.

4. What four words relate to being small?
   a.
   b.
   c.
   d.

Roots Practice

1. There are four words in this lesson that have the "pel" root. What are they?
   a.
   b.
   c.
   d.

2. Based on these words, what do you think the root "pel" means?

3. There are two words with the grac/grat root in our word list. What are they?
   a.
   b.

4. Based on these words, what do you think the grac/grat root means?

5. Can you think of any other words that have the grac/grat root?

Synonyms Practice

1. ASTOUND:
   (A) detain
   (B) joke
   (C) result
   (D) stun

2. DAINTY:
   (A) costly
   (B) delicate
   (C) flustered
   (D) sudden

3. IMMENSE:
   (A) colossal
   (B) modern
   (C) popular
   (D) restricted

4. MEAGER:
   (A) humane
   (B) intricate
   (C) scant
   (D) thick

5. PROPEL:
   (A) baffle
   (B) make
   (C) push
   (D) retire

Sentence Completion Practice

1. The high, snow-covered peaks of the Himalayan Mountains cause visitors to remember the ------- of the mountains long after the tourists have returned home.
   (A) astonishment
   (B) majesty
   (C) path
   (D) sunshine

2. Despite the fact that he was a famous singer, Elvis Presley was ------- to serve in the armed forces.
   (A) bewildered
   (B) compelled
   (C) remained
   (D) vanished

3. The cardinal and blue jay are very similar in size but the blue jay is --------larger.
   (A) authentically
   (B) graciously
   (C) nobly
   (D) slightly

4. In order to reduce disease caused by mosquitoes, park rangers recommend using DEET to ------- insects.
   (A) express
   (B) magnify
   (C) repel
   (D) utilize

5. When a neighbor gave Jim a cup of flour to finish his cake, he returned the measuring cup with candies in it as a sign of ---------.
   (A) gratitude
   (B) isolation
   (C) learning
   (D) petition

6. In the process of making peanut butter, the extra oil is often ------- to keep it from collecting on top of the peanut butter.
   (A) expelled
   (B) fooled
   (C) grown
   (D) portrayed

Lesson Eight Answers

Word List Practice

1. a. baffle
   b. astound
   c. astonishment
   d. bewilder
   e. stun
2. fluster
3. a. colossal
   b. immense
   c. magnify
   d. majesty
4. a. dainty
   b. scant
   c. slight
   d. meager

Roots Practice

1. a. compel
   b. expel
   c. propel
   d. repel
2. to drive or urge
3. a. gracious
   b. gratitude
4. to be thankful
5. the words grace, graceful, and grateful all have the grac/grat root

Synonyms Practice

1. D
2. B
3. A
4. C
5. C

Sentence Completion Practice

1. B
2. B
3. D
4. C
5. A
6. A

Lesson Nine

Words to Learn

Below are the twenty words used in Lesson Nine; refer back to this list as needed as you move through the lesson.

Durable: long-lasting
Incredible: unbelievable
Belittle: criticize
Decree: order (given by someone in a position of power)
Jilt: reject

Endure: to last (or get through something)
Credible: believable
Sneer: to laugh at
Pardon: forgive
Valiant: courageous

Duration: period (of time)
Begrudge: envy
Gloat: boast
Preside: rule over
Gallant: brave

Jeer: ridicule (put down)
Reek: stink
Mock: make fun of
Proclaim: declare
Noble: honorable

Word List Practice

1. What five words relate to just being plain mean to another person?
   a.
   b.
   c.
   d.
   e.

2. If your friend bragged about getting a brand new boat, what would he be doing?

3. If you really wanted your own boat, what might you do?

4. If a person does this, no one would want to sit next to him or her on an airplane.

5. A president might do these four things. A really annoying person might also try to do these things.
   a.
   b.
   c.
   d.

6. These three words could be used to describe the Knights of the Round Table:
   a.
   b.
   c.

Roots Practice

1. What three words in our list have the "dur" root?
   a.
   b.
   c.

2. From the meanings of these three words, what do you think the "dur" root means?

3. There are two words in our list that have the "cred" root. What are they?
   a.
   b.

4. Based on these words, what do you think that the "cred" root means?

Synonyms Practice

1. BELITTLE:
   (A) crowd
   (B) hope
   (C) mock
   (D) tie

2. JILT:
   (A) endure
   (B) note
   (C) proceed
   (D) reject

3. INCREDIBLE:
   (A) durable
   (B) kind
   (C) plump
   (D) unbelievable

4. GLOAT:
   (A) boast
   (B) lead
   (C) nod
   (D) reek

5. VALIANT:
   (A) cultural
   (B) gallant
   (C) punctual
   (D) slender

Sentence Completion Practice

1. Before the French Revolution, if a king or queen ------- that something must become law, then the law was automatically passed.
   (A) decreed
   (B) jilted
   (C) reduced
   (D) silenced

2. In a court case, it is important that lawyers find witnesses that are --------.
   (A) astonished
   (B) credible
   (C) pardoned
   (D) scattered

3. Due to their kingly appearance, lions are often considered the most ------- of the animal kingdom.
   (A) begrudged
   (B) flattered
   (C) hopeful
   (D) noble

4. The Vice President is technically supposed to ------- over the Senate, but in reality a senator often takes over the leadership duties for the Senate.
   (A) fascinate
   (B) jeer
   (C) preside
   (D) sneer

5. The flight attendant often asks passengers to turn off their electronic devices for the ------- of the flight, or until the airplane lands.
   (A) cabin
   (B) duration
   (C) manager
   (D) proclamation

Lesson Nine Answers

Word List Practice

1. a. belittle
   b. jeer
   c. jilt
   d. sneer
   e. mock
2. gloating
3. begrudge him
4. reek
5. a. preside
   b. decree
   c. pardon
   d. proclaim
6. a. valiant
   b. noble
   c. gallant

Roots Practice

1. a. durable
   b. endure
   c. duration
2. to last
3. a. incredible
   b. credible
4. to believe

Synonyms Practice

1. C
2. D
3. D
4. A
5. B

Sentence Completion Practice

1. A
2. B
3. D
4. C
5. B

Lesson Ten

Words to Learn

Below are the twenty words used in Lesson Ten; refer back to this list as needed as you move through the lesson.

Overcome: conquer
Superior: better
Reside: live in
Bleak: hopeless
Prominent: well-known

Treacherous: dangerous
Overlook: miss (not see)
Menace: threat
Dwell: occupy (live in)
Inhabitant: resident (someone who lives in a place)

Culprit: criminal (guilty person)
Overdue: late
Rascal: villain (person who is up to no good)
Supreme: best
Notable: important

Superb: excellent
Abode: home
Dreary: gloomy
Overtake: pass
Distinguished: famous

Word List Practice

1. What four words from our list have to do with where someone lives?
   a.
   b.
   c.
   d.

2. When you go on a trip, what three words do you NOT want to use to describe it?
   a.
   b.
   c.

3. What three words describe someone who is well-known?
   a.
   b.
   c.

4. What three words might you use to describe someone who gets in trouble or breaks the law?
   a.
   b.
   c.

Roots Practice

1. What four words in our list have the root "over"?
   a.
   b.
   c.
   d.

2. What is the difference between the words overcome and overtake?

3. What three words in our list have the super/supr root?

   a.

   b.

   c.

4. Based on these words, what do you think the super/supr root means?

Synonyms Practice

1. RESIDE:
   (A) dwell
   (B) feed
   (C) miss
   (D) walk

2. DISTINGUISHED:
   (A) bleak
   (B) final
   (C) notable
   (D) thrilling

3. ABODE:
   (A) drop
   (B) home
   (C) menace
   (D) town

4. RASCAL:
   (A) culprit
   (B) filter
   (C) mystery
   (D) smear

5. BLEAK:
   (A) clear
   (B) dreary
   (C) supreme
   (D) talkative

Sentence Completion Practice

1. Albert Einstein was ------- during his lifetime since he was well-known for discovering the theory of relativity.
   (A) believable
   (B) hidden
   (C) overlooked
   (D) prominent

2. The Cliffs of Moher have a reputation for being -------- because there is a steep drop-off to the ocean hundreds of feet below.
    (A) essential
    (B) limber
    (C) overdue
    (D) treacherous

3. The author Charles Dickens was perhaps one of the most well-known -------- of London.
    (A) arrivals
    (B) inhabitants
    (C) nicknames
    (D) sparrows

4. Diarist Anne Frank was able to ------ the fact that she was essentially a prisoner in an attic and write one of the best-selling books of all times.
    (A) avoid
    (B) browse
    (C) overcome
    (D) travel

5. Even late in an election, it is still possible for one candidate to --------- another candidate.
    (A) overtake
    (B) stagger
    (C) trouble
    (D) yelp

6. People travelled for many miles to taste the -------- food at a local restaurant.
    (A) corrupt
    (B) hazardous
    (C) superb
    (D) warm

Answers to Lesson Ten

Word List Practice

1. a. dwell
   b. reside
   c. inhabitant
   d. abode
2. a. bleak
   b. treacherous
   c. dreary
3. a. notable
   b. prominent
   c. distinguished
4. a. rascal
   b. menace
   c. culprit

Roots Practice

1. a. overcome
   b. overtake
   c. overlook
   d. overdue
2. When we use the word overcome, we tend to be talking about defeating something that is not another competitor. For example, a person might overcome stuttering. When we us the word overtake, we tend to be talking about passing a single competitor. For example, we might say that a bicycle rider overtakes another rider during a race.

3. a. superior
   b. supreme
   c. superb
4. above or beyond

Synonyms Practice

1. A
2. C
3. B
4. A
5. B

Sentence Completion Practice

1. D
2. D
3. B
4. C
5. A
6. C

ISEE Reading Comprehension Section

In the ISEE reading section, you are given passages and then asked questions about these passages. There are five passages in the reading comprehension section and each passage has five questions. For the entire section, there will be a total of twenty-five questions. You will have twenty-five minutes to complete the section. There will be only one reading section on your test.

- 5 passages
- 5 questions for each passage
- 25 total questions
- 25 minutes to complete section
- Only one reading section

You may be thinking, "I know how to read, I am good on this section." However, most people applying to independent schools know how to read. In order to get around the 50th percentile score for fifth graders on the reading section, you need to answer a little more than half of the questions correctly. This means that half the fifth graders taking this test are getting less than that.

- To get the median score for 5th grade, you need to answer a little more than half of the questions correctly

The issue is that not every student can get a perfect score on the reading section, so the test writers have to create a test where some students who know how to read are going to miss several questions.

So how do the test writers get you to answer so many questions incorrectly? First of all, the questions can be very detail oriented. Think of this not as a reading test, but as looking for a needle in a haystack- with very little time to find it. Secondly, they include answer choices that take the words from the passage, but those words are describing something else. Students often see these answer choices and think that if the words show up in the passage, it must be the correct answer. However, the words do not apply to that particular question. Lastly, they use your own brain against you! How do they do this?? They include answer choices that would be a logical conclusion, but are not mentioned in the passage, so they are wrong.

- Very detail-oriented questions
- Test writers take words from another part of the passage and put them in the incorrect answer choices
- Some answer choices are logical conclusions, but aren't mentioned in the passage so they are not correct

By making a plan and sticking to it, however, you can overcome these obstacles and beat the average score- by a lot!

In this section, first we will cover the general plan of attack and then we will get into the details that make the difference.

Reading section plan of attack

Students can significantly improve their reading scores by following an easy plan:

Step 1: Plan your time.
You have five minutes per passage, so be sure to lay out your time before you begin.

Step 2: Prioritize passages.
Play to your strengths. Don't just answer the passages in the order that they appear.

Step 3: Go to the questions first.
Mark questions as either specific or general. You want to know what to look for as you read.

Step 4: Read the passage.
If you run across the answer to a specific question, go ahead and answer that. But do not worry if you don't see an answer on the first read through.

Step 5: Answer specific questions.
If there are any specific questions that you did not answer yet, go back and find the answers.

Step 6: Answer general questions.
Answer any questions that ask about the passage as a whole.

Step 7: Repeat steps 3-6 with next passage.

    You've got it under control. Just keep cranking through the section until you are done.

Keep in mind that this section is not a test of how well you read. It is a test of how well you test. You need to manage your time and think about the process.

Step #1- Plan your time

Before you do anything, take thirty seconds to plan out your time. You have five minutes per passage, and there are five passages.

- 5 minutes per passage

Look at the starting time and make a quick chart of when you should finish each passage at the top of your first page. For example, let's say you start at 9:23, then your chart should look like this

Start- 9:23
1 - 9:28
2 - 9:33
3 - 9:38
4 - 9:43
5 - 9:48

We make a chart like this because we won't be answering the passages in the order that they appear. You don't have to follow the pacing chart exactly, but you should be close. If you finish the first passage in 2 minutes, then you are moving way too quickly. If it takes you 7 minutes to finish the first passage, then you will know that you need to speed up.

- Timing chart is a rough guideline

Drill #1

Let's say you start a reading section and the start time is 9:32. Fill in the chart below:

Start-

1-

2-

3-

4-

5-

(Answers to this drill are found on p. 128)

Step #2- Prioritize passages

Take a quick look at your passages. You can even quickly read the first sentence to get an idea of what the passage is about. If you see a passage with a topic that you have studied in school, do that first. While you do not need any background information to answer the passage questions, it is easier to understand what is going on quickly if you are familiar with the topic. If there are any passages that stick out as being really long, save those for last.

- Look for passages with a familiar topic
- Save really long passages for last

The following are the types of passages that you may see:

Narrative

These passages read like a story. The story may be true or it may be fiction. Some of the types of narrative that you may see include biographical narrative (tells a story about a historical figure), personal narrative (an author shares an experience he or she has had), or fictional narrative (a made-up story). These passages tend to have more questions that require drawing a conclusion or figuring out what is implied.

- In the form of a story
- Can be fiction or non-fiction
- Questions tend to be more about drawing conclusions and figuring out what is implied

Expository

Expository passages explain something. The goal of an expository passage is to explain, not to tell a story. You may see passages that compare and contrast, describe a historical event, or explain a scientific occurrence. The questions for these passages tend to be more detail-oriented.

- Explain something
- Questions more detail oriented

Persuasive

These passages are designed to convince the reader of something. Persuasive passages may offer an opinion, give pros and cons, or present a problem and a solution. Questions for these types of passages tend to require following an argument or deciding which evidence supports the argument.

- Convince the reader
- Questions may ask reader to follow an argument or decide which evidence supports an argument

Descriptive

The purpose of descriptive passages is to describe something so clearly that it creates a picture in the reader's mind. Questions for descriptive passages tend to test details since the passage is mainly composed of details.

- Creates a picture in your mind

- Questions are very detail oriented

So what passage types should you answer first? That depends on what you are good at! If you are good at finding picky details, then the expository or descriptive passages might be better for you. If inferring ideas and understanding arguments is your strength, then persuasive or narrative passages may be easier for you. In general, you want to do passages that are easier for you first and save the toughest one for the end.

- Different people will find different passages easy or hard
- Do the passages that are easier for you first

You start the reading section. After a quick scan of each passage, you have to prioritize the order of answering the passages. Quickly number the passages below in the order that you would answer them.

Passage topics:

Passage about the invention of the unicycle: #_____

Essay about the importance of school nutrition: #_____

Description of the creation of the first American Flag: #_____

Passage about why we have Leap Day: #_____

Passage from a novel #_____

(Answers to this drill are found on p. 128)

Step #3- When you start a passage, go to questions first

It is important that you identify specific (S) and general (G) questions before you begin to read. You may come across the answer to a specific question as you read, so you also want to underline what the question is asking about for specific questions.

- Mark general questions with a G
- Mark specific questions with an S
- For specific questions, make sure you underline what the question is about if it references a particular topic

So how do you know if a question will be specific or general? Become familiar with the question types below.

General Questions

On the ISEE, you will see the following types of questions that are general:

- Mark these question types with a G

1. Main Idea Questions

These questions ask you for the overall theme of the passage.

Here are some examples:

- The primary purpose of this passage is to
- Which of the following best states the passage's main idea?
- This passage is mainly concerned with

Main idea questions are definitely general questions. You should mark them with a G for general and remember to answer them after any specific questions.

- Mark main idea questions with a G for general
- Answer them at the end

2. Organization Questions

Organization questions ask you to look for the structure of the passage and see how the parts all fit together.

Here is what they look like:

- The function of the second paragraph is to
- Which of the following would be most logical for the author to discuss next?

These are general questions, so mark them with a G. These questions want you to look at the passage as a whole. To tackle these questions, write a word or two next to each paragraph that summarizes what that paragraph is about. Look at these labels to see the flow of the passage. From this, you should be able to figure out how one paragraph functions in the passage or what would make sense to discuss next. Don't worry too much about these questions, you may see only a couple of them on the entire reading section.

- Mark organization questions with a G
- Answer them at the end
- Jot down a word or two next to each paragraph so that you can see the structure of the passage as a whole
- There won't be very many of these questions, don't worry too much about them

3. Tone or Attitude Questions

These questions ask you to identify the tone of a piece or writer or how the writer feels about something.

They might look like these:

- Which best expresses the author's attitude about (some topic)?
- The tone of the passage can best be described as

These are general questions, so we mark them with a G. In general, we look for moderate answers for these questions. An author is not likely to be "enraged" on the ISEE, but they might be "annoyed". This is the least common question type on the reading section- you might only see one of them!

- Mark tone or attitude questions with a G
- Look for moderate answers
- Least common question type in the whole reading section

Specific Questions

There are also question types for specific questions:

- Remember to mark specific questions with an S
- If there is a key word in a specific question (i.e. what the question is asking about), be sure to underline it

4. Supporting Idea Questions

These questions are looking for details.

Here are some examples:

- The passage states that which of the following people helped Johnny Appleseed?
- Which question is answered by the passage?
- Which statement about the spring equinox is supported by the passage?

These questions are definitely specific questions. They are looking for details from the passage that are directly stated and not asking you to pull together information from different places. For these questions, you should be able to underline the correct answer restated word-for-word in the passage.

- Mark supporting idea questions with an S for specific
- You should be able to underline the correct answer in the passage

5. Inference Questions

Inference questions ask you to draw a conclusion from the text. They might ask you how two ideas or people compare, to interpret what the author states, or to predict what might happen.

Here are some examples of inference questions:

- Charles Dickens clearly believed
- According to the passage, both Susan B. Anthony and Elizabeth Cady Stanton
- In the second paragraph, the author implies
- Which of the following best characterizes bacterial growth as the passage describes it?

These are specific questions because you will find the answer in just small portion of the passage. Mark these questions with an S and remember that you must be able to underline the answer in the passage.

Inference questions are one of the most common question types on the ISEE. The key to these questions is that you may not be able to underline just one sentence in the passage that contains your answer, but you should be able to underline the evidence for the correct answer.

- Mark inference questions with an S
- Underline the evidence in the passage for the correct answer- it may show up in more than one place but you should be able to underline all of it
- Practice these questions- they show up a lot!

6. Vocabulary Questions

These questions ask you to use the context of the passage to figure out what a word means.

Here are some examples:

- In line 14, the word "capable" most nearly means
- In line 25, "captivate" most nearly means to

These are specific questions because they require you to use just a small part of the passage. You cannot underline the correct answer for these questions, however. For vocabulary questions, we have a different approach. We actually find the word in the passage, cross it out, and then plug in the answer choices to see what makes sense in that sentence. It is important that you practice this strategy- vocabulary questions are one of the most common questions types in the reading section. In fact, there is usually a vocabulary question for every single passage.

- Mark vocabulary questions with an S
- Cross out the word in the passage and then fill in answer choices to see what has the same meaning as the question word
- Get good at vocabulary questions- there is one on almost every passage!

As you can see, there are definitely more specific questions than general questions on the ISEE reading section.

To practice identifying whether questions are specific or general, complete the drills below by identifying each question as general or specific. Time yourself on each drill to see how you improve! If you aren't completely sure of whether a question is specific or general, don't get too worried or spend a lot of time on that. The goal of this strategy is to save time in the long run and it is easy to change your mind as you work through a passage.

Drill #3

1. This passage is primarily about

2. As used in line 7, "graciously" most nearly means

3. It can be inferred from the passage that which statement about types of grasses is true?

4. According to the passage, how long did it take to travel across the country on the first transcontinental railway?

5. The author's style is best described as

Time:

Drill #4

1. The door to the barn was probably made from

2. The sounds referred to in the passage were

3. According to the author, the musicians stopped playing because

4. An "emu" is probably a type of

5. The tone of this passage can best be described as

Time:

Drill #5

1. The sound that came from the floorboards can best be described as

2. It can be inferred that from the passage that early settlers did not have windows in their homes because

3. What made the citizens call a town meeting?

4. As it is used in line 15, the word "substantial" most nearly means

5. Which of the following questions is answered by information in the passage?

Time:

Drill #6

1. Which of the following best states the main idea of the passage?

2. In line 4, John Adams' use of the word "furious" is ironic for which of the following reasons?

3. How does Adams' speech reflect the idea that government is "for the people, by the people"?

4. The purpose of Adams' speech was to

5. Why does Adams use the word "mocking" in line 13?

Time:

(Answers to drills 3-6 are found on p. 128)

Step #4- Read the passage

Now, you can go ahead and read the passage. If you happen to run across the answer to one of your specific questions, go ahead and answer it. If not, don't worry about it.

You have to be a little zen about looking for the answers while you read. You can spend five minutes obsessing over finding the answer for one particular question, but if you just move on, you are likely to come across the answer later.

- It's a little like love, sometimes you just have to let it go and trust that it will come back to you

Step #5- Answer specific questions

After you finish reading, answer any specific questions that you have not yet answered. For these questions, think of it as a treasure hunt. The right answer is there, you just have to find it. Generally, you should be able to underline the exact answer paraphrased in the passage or evidence for the correct answer. If you can't do that, you just haven't found it yet. Keep looking. You should also think about what category the question fits into (we will work on those in just a minute).

When you are looking for the answer to a specific question, skim! Don't read every word, you have already done that. Look quickly for the words that you underlined in the question. Also, remember our old friend ruling out.

- Skim when looking for the answers for specific questions
- Use ruling out
- For specific questions, you should be able to underline the correct answer restated in the passage or evidence for the correct answer
- Think about what category questions fit into

Now, we are going to work on practicing strategies for each particular type of specific question.

On the following page is a passage that can be used for all of the question type practice drills. Go ahead and tear this passage out from the book. We want you to develop good habits of underlining and marking the passages, which is hard to do if you are flipping back and forth.

Passage for Drills 7-12

1 One night, I looked out my kitchen window and saw a black and white cat ambling across
2 my lawn. I thought that it might be injured, so I grabbed a flashlight and went outside.
3 When I saw two more black and white cats squeeze out from under the porch, I realized
4 that they weren't cats at all: they were skunks. I stood very still and watched the three
5 skunks shuffle around the corner of the house. Sighing with relief, I found a heavy rock
6 and positioned it in front of the hole under the porch wall. Satisfied, I went back inside.
7
8 The next morning, I went outside to inspect my handiwork. Kneeling down, I saw fresh
9 marks in the dirt, and a new hole next to the rock. Of course the rock didn't stop the
10 skunks from going back under the porch. Their sharp claws are made for digging, and
11 when they found the rock in their way, they simply excavated a new hole.
12
13 I wasn't sure what to do about my new neighbors. I didn't want to hurt them, but I
14 certainly didn't want them residing under my porch. I considered digging the dirt away
15 from the bottom of the porch walls, and then attaching plywood extending below ground
16 level. I realized, however, that I couldn't do this unless I knew that no skunks were still
17 under the porch. Because skunks are nocturnal, I would need to do the job after dark
18 when they were out looking for food.
19
20 Finally, I decided to ignore the skunks. I made sure that I kept my garbage cans sealed
21 tightly because I didn't want make my visitors too comfortable by providing them with
22 free meals. I haven't seen the skunks for a while, and I don't know whether they are still
23 living under the porch or have moved on. Either way, my policy of benign neglect had
24 the intended outcome: I don't bother the skunks, and they don't bother me.

This page left intentionally blank so that passage can be removed from book to use for drills.

Supporting Idea Questions

As mentioned above, supporting idea questions are looking for a picky detail. When you read through this type of question, you want to underline specifically what the question is asking about. For example, if the question is "How many years did it take for the transcontinental railroad to be built?", you would underline "how many years". The whole passage is probably about the transcontinental railroad, so underlining that would not help you pinpoint where to find the answer.

- Underline the detail in the question that will tell you where to find your answer, if appropriate

Some supporting ideas questions do not have a detail to underline. For example, questions such as "Which question is answered by the passage?" and "Which statement is supported by the passage?" do not have a detail in the question that we can skim for.

- Not every supporting idea question has something to underline in the question

The key to answering this type of question is to underline the correct answer restated in the passage. If you can't do that, you simply have not yet found the answer- keep looking!

- Correct answer can be underlined in the passage

The following is a drill for practicing this type of question. The questions refer to the passage about skunks.

We want to be sure that you develop good habits. So what are good habits for supporting idea questions?

- Underline in the question what it is asking about (if appropriate)
- Underline the evidence for the correct answer in the passage

Drill #7

1. The author placed a rock in front of the porch wall in order to
   (A) mark where the skunks come and go.
   (B) block the opening so that the skunks could not go under the porch.
   (C) make it easier for the skunks to find their home.
   (D) add decoration to the porch wall.

2. Which of the following questions is answered by the passage?
   (A) What type of food do skunks prefer?
   (B) What was the author's porch wall made of?
   (C) What time of day are skunks active?
   (D) Do the skunks still live under the author's porch?

(Answers to this drill are found on p. 128)

Inference Questions

On the ISEE, inference questions ask you to draw conclusions from what the author has written. These questions often use the words "implies", "it can be inferred", and the "the author suggests".

- If you see the words infer, imply, or suggest, it is probably an inference question

The trick to these questions is that they aren't looking for some deep conclusion. They are not asking you to read into a character's motivation or determine what another person thinks or feels. That would be too hard for a multiple-choice test! The correct answer for this type of question is the answer choice that has the most evidence in the passage. Also, look for answers that are less extreme. For example, an author is more likely to suggest that an animal is a pest than suggest that an animal should be completely eliminated.

- Look for the answer choice with the most evidence
- Look for less extreme answers

For the following drill, use the passage about skunks to answer the questions. Remember to underline evidence for the correct answer.

- Underline evidence in the passage

1. When the author says, "my policy of benign neglect had the intended outcome", he or she is suggesting
   (A) the skunks are no longer bothering the author.
   (B) the skunks have definitely left the area under the porch.
   (C) there are now more skunks under the porch.
   (D) skunks are known for eating out of unsecured trash cans.

2. When the author considers "attaching plywood extending below ground level", the author is implying
   (A) that skunks are nocturnal.
   (B) the skunks are annoying to him.
   (C) the skunks would go around the plywood.
   (D) the skunks would not be able to dig through the plywood to get under his porch.

(Answers to this drill are found on p. 128)

Vocabulary Questions

On the ISEE reading section, they test whether or not you can use context to figure out the meaning of a word. The words tend to be higher-level words that you may not know the definition of.

The best way to answer these questions is to go back to the passage and actually cross out the word that the question asks about. Then plug the answer choices into that space in the sentence and see which answer choice gives you the same meaning.

- Cross out word in passage
- Plug in answer choices to see what makes sense

For the following drill, use the skunk passage. Remember to physically cross out the word-don't just do it in your head!

1. In line 11, the word "excavated" most nearly means
   (A) smelled.
   (B) dug.
   (C) closed.
   (D) ate.

2. In line 1, the word "ambling" most nearly means
   (A) rolling.
   (B) sleeping.
   (C) looking.
   (D) walking.

(Answers to this drill are found on p. 129)

Step #6- Answer general questions

After answering the specific questions, you have probably reread the passage multiple times. The trick for the general questions is not to get bogged down by the details, however. How do we do this? By rereading the last sentence of the entire passage before we answer general questions. This will clarify the main idea.

- Reread last sentence of passage before answering general questions

Main Idea Questions

Main idea questions are looking for you to identify what the passage is about. You can identify them because they often use the words main or primarily.

- Often have the words "main" or "primarily" in them

The trick to main idea questions on the ISEE is that incorrect answers are often details from the passage. Students see these answer choices, remembering reading about that detail, and then choose that answer because it shows up in the passage. The problem is that these answers are a detail from the passage and not the main idea.

- Wrong answer choices are often details from the passage

For the following drill, use the skunk passage. Remember to practice good habits:

- Reread the last sentence before answering a general question
- Don't choose a detail from the passage

 Drill #10

1. The primary purpose of this passage is to
   (A) explain the sleeping patterns of skunks.
   (B) explore the differences between skunks and cats.
   (C) relate the experience of one person with skunks.
   (D) compare different methods of skunk extermination.

(The answer to this drill is found on p. 129)

Organization Questions

Organization questions ask about why an author has chosen to include a particular part of the passage or ask about what the author would discuss next. These questions are testing your ability to see the organization of the passage or the function of a particular section.

To answer these questions, jot down a word or two next to each paragraph that summarizes what that paragraph is about. Look for the flow and what each paragraph contributes.

- Jot down a word or two next to each paragraph
- Look at these labels to see how the pieces fit together

1. The primary purpose of the first two sentences is
   (A) to introduce a sense of suspense to keep the reader interested.
   (B) to summarize previous research.
   (C) to introduce an argument.
   (D) to provide the setting for a story.

2. Which topic is the author most likely to discuss next?
   (A) How to deal with cockroaches.
   (B) The growth of the skunk population in urban areas.
   (C) The reappearance of skunks in the next season.
   (D) What the skunks are named.

(Answers to this drill are found on p. 129)

Tone or Attitude Questions

Tone or attitude questions on the ISEE ask you to draw your own conclusion about how the author approaches the topic. Are they annoyed? Trying to be informative?

Since these are general questions, we want to reread the last sentence before we answer them. It is also particularly important to use ruling out on these questions. Remember that we are looking for the "best" answer, which in some cases might just be the least wrong answer choice.

- Reread last sentence
- Use ruling out

There are a couple of tricks to these types of questions. First of all, look for moderate answers. For example, the test writers are not likely to choose a writer that is either ecstatic (extremely happy) or enraged (really, really mad). Also, don't be afraid of words that you do not know! Just because you don't know what the word "objective" means doesn't mean that it can't be the right answer.

- Look for moderate answers
- Don't avoid answer choices with words that you do not know

Finally, if it is a tone question, think about what type of writing the passage is. A fiction passage might have a tone that is lively, nervous, excited, etc. A non-fiction passage might have a tone that is objective, informative, interested, etc.

- If it is a tone question, think about what would be appropriate for fiction or non-fiction

The following drill refers to the skunk passage.

1. Which best expresses the author's attitude about the skunks under his porch?
   (A) outraged
   (B) not overly concerned
   (C) joyous
   (D) tired

(The answer to this drill is found on p. 129)

Step #7- Move on to your next passage and repeat!

When you complete a passage, check your time against the chart you created before starting the section and then move on to the next passage.

- Keep track of time
- Just keep on truckin'

A note about what types of answers to look for

On the ISEE, the test writers have to make sure that not everyone gets a perfect score. As a matter of fact, they have to make sure that students who are good readers still miss several questions.

The art of answering reading questions correctly often comes down to:

- On general questions, be sure not to pick a detail as an answer
- On specific questions, watch out for answer choices that take words from the passage but change them slightly so that the meaning is different

Secret #1: On general questions, be sure not to pick an answer that is a detail

The test writers need students to miss general questions. Usually if a student sees an answer choice that was mentioned in the passage, this answer choice will be really tempting! These answer choices are wrong, however, because they are details and not the main idea. The best way to focus in on the real main idea is to reread the last sentence before answering a general question.

- Look out for answers that are details- these are the wrong answers for main idea questions
- Reread the last sentence before answering a general question

Below is a short passage followed by a general question. See if you can pick out the answers that are tricks!

Drill #13

1 In the late 1870's, King David Kalakaua sat in his palace in Honolulu
2 reading by the light of a gas lamp. At that time, there were no electric
3 lights in Honolulu, Hawaii. As a matter of fact, there were very few
4 electric lights in the world.
5
6 It wasn't until 1879 that Thomas Edison invented a filament light bulb
7 that could burn for 40 hours. There were other light bulbs before this
8 but they burned out too quickly to be practical. Thomas Edison's new
9 light bulb changed everything.
10
11 After reading about this new light bulb and its inventor, King Kalakaua
12 decided that he must meet this great inventor. In 1881 he had the
13 chance. King Kalakaua was on a world tour and met with Edison in
14 New York.
15
16 It took five long years before a light bulb shined in the palace. On July
17 26, 1886, a demonstration of the new electric light was held at the
18 palace. It was a huge event with a tea party thrown by two princesses.
19 The military band played and troops marched to celebrate.
20
21 After the exhibit, a power plant was built on the palace grounds that
22 could power more than just one light. On Friday, March 23, 1888,
23 Princess Kaiulani threw the switch and turned on the new power
24 system. In that moment, Iolani Palace officially became the first royal
25 residence in the world to be lit by electricity. Electricity had come to
26 the Hawaiian Islands.

1. The primary purpose of this passage is to
   (A) describe the friendship between King Kalakaua and Thomas Edison.
   (B) explain why Thomas Edison's lightbulb was better than the light
       bulbs that came before it.
   (C) relate how the Hawaiian islands came to have electricity.
   (D) show how much King David Kalakaua cared for his people.

What is the correct answer? Which answer choices were tricks?

(The answer to this drill is found on p. 129)

Secret #2: On specific questions, watch out for answer choices that have words from the passage

On the ISEE, answer choices often have words from the passage, but they might have inserted another word or two so that the meaning is different. Some answer choices also have words from the passage, but they are not the correct answer to that particular question.

- Be cautious when choosing an answer that repeats words from the passage

Here is an example. Let's say that the passage states:

John was upset when Sam got into the car with Trish.

The question may look something like:

1. Which of the following is implied by the author?
   (A) John was upset with Trish when he got into the car.
   (B) Sam and Trish were upset when John got into the car.
   (C) John and Sam were cousins.
   (D) John was not happy because Sam rode with Trish.

Answer choices A and B use words from the passage, but do not have the same meaning as what the passage says. Choice C is just unrelated- which happens on the ISEE! Choice D restates what the passage says.

In the drill below, there is a sentence from a passage. There is then a list of answer choices. You have to decide whether the answer choice has the same meaning as the passage, or whether the words have been twisted around to mean something else.

Drill #14

Passage: When the morning sun rose high above the horizon, a small boy could be spotted as he carried a bucket along the ridge of a hill in the distance.

Answer state:	Same meaning	Twisted meaning
1. A small boy was spotted along the horizon, looking almost like a bucket on the hill.		
2. Along the ridge, a child was carrying a pail in the morning.		
3. The small boy spotted the sun rising over a ridge as he carried a bucket.		
4. Far away, it was possible to see a boy carrying a bucket as he walked along the top of a hill in the morning sun.		

(Answers to this drill are found on p. 129)

We are going to finish up the reading section with a full passage.

Remember to apply what we have learned.

What are the good habits that we are looking for?

1. Mark questions S (specific) or G (general) before looking at passage.
2. Answer specific questions first.
3. Underline the correct answer for specific questions.
4. Reread the last sentence before answering general questions.
5. Rule out any answer choices that are details for general questions.

Drill #15

1 When I was in third grade my class took a field trip to Colonial
2 Williamsburg. When our teacher, Miss Beverly, told us about the trip, we
3 were all very excited. Colonial Williamsburg was a two-hour bus ride away.
4 We had never been to a place so exotic.
5
6 I was particularly excited because Catherine Cleary had promised to sit
7 next to me on the bus. I was new to the school and Catherine was the
8 most popular girl in the third grade. Every day she matched the ribbons
9 on her shoes to the ribbons in her hair. I felt like royalty to be asked to sit
10 next to such perfection.
11
12 On the day of the trip, we woke up to pouring rain. I was very worried.
13 Would the trip be cancelled? My mother assured me that it would not.
14
15 I got ready for school keeping the weather in mind. After much debate, I
16 put on my thick yellow rain boots. I wanted to match my hair ribbons to
17 my shoe ribbons, but I did not actually have any shoes with ribbons. I
18 decided that bright yellow boots were second best.
19
20 I put on a thick sweater since it can be cold on rainy days. I also pulled on
21 wool tights. It would be a very long ride in an unheated school bus and I
22 didn't want Catherine to think that I hadn't planned.
23
24 We got to school and quickly loaded the bus for our long journey.
25 Catherine held my hand as we boarded. I wanted to sit near the front since
26 I was prone to getting carsick. Catherine told me the cool kids sat in the
27 back, though. I didn't dare object.
28
29 The bus ride started out uneventfully. However, about a half hour into the
30 ride the sun came out. Suddenly, the temperature in the bus rose rapidly.
31 I had planned for a bus that would not be heated. I hadn't counted on the
32 fact that the bus would not be cooled, either. There was no way to take off
33 my warm tights. I had not thought to bring extra shoes, so the boots also
34 had to stay.
35
36 As we rode along, I got warmer and warmer. And the bumps in the back
37 of the bus got bigger and bigger. I was green long before we got to Colonial
38 Williamsburg. Needless to say, Catherine Cleary never asked me to sit next
39 to her again.

Drill #15

1. This passage is mainly concerned with
    (A) providing advice for planning a fieldtrip to Colonial Williamsburg.
    (B) relating the experience of one student.
    (C) how to dress appropriately on rainy days.
    (D) stressing the importance of fieldtrips.

2. In line 27, the word "object" most nearly means
    (A) disagree.
    (B) ask.
    (C) drive.
    (D) ride.

3. What can be inferred from the last paragraph (lines 36-39)
    (A) It was raining when the students arrived at Colonial Williamsburg.
    (B) No one wanted to sit next to Catherine Cleary.
    (C) The narrator had to leave the fieldtrip early.
    (D) The narrator became sick on the bus ride.

4. Information from the passage could be used to answer which question?
    (A) How many students were on the trip?
    (B) Where is Colonial Williamsburg?
    (C) What grade was Catherine Cleary in?
    (D) What was the weather like in Colonial Williamsburg?

5. According to the story, the narrator did not want to sit in the back of the bus because
    (A) she did not think she was popular enough to sit in the back.
    (B) she was concerned that she might become ill from the motion.
    (C) it was too hot in the back of the bus.
    (D) she didn't like Catherine Cleary.

Be sure to check your answers and figure out WHY you missed any questions that you answered incorrectly.

Answers to drills

Drill #1

Start- 9:32

1-9:37

2-9:42

3-9:47

4-9:52

5-9:57

Drill #2

There is no right order to answer the passages for everyone. It depends upon what you find interesting! If you find the passage interesting, you are likely to pick up on a lot more of the details.

Drill #3

1. G
2. S
3. S
4. S
5. G

Drill #4

1. S
2. S
3. S
4. S
5. G

Drill #5

1. S
2. S
3. S
4. S
5. S

Drill #6

1. G
2. S
3. S or G- it depends on that the whole passage is about. Remember, we have to stay flexible when we do this.
4. G
5. S

Drill #7

1. B
2. C

Drill #8

1. A
2. D

Drill #9

1. B
2. D

Drill #10

1. C

Drill #11

1. A
2. C

Drill #12

1. B

Drill #13

1. Choice C is the correct answer
   choice. Choices A and B are traps-
   they are details but not the main idea.

Drill #14

1. Twisted meaning
2. Same meaning
3. Twisted meaning
4. Same meaning

Drill #15

1. B
2. A
3. D
4. C
5. B

Quantitative Reasoning and Mathematics Achievement

On the ISEE, there are two math sections. One is Quantitative Reasoning and the other is Mathematics Achievement. There are no open response math questions on the ISEE- they are all multiple-choice.

- Two math sections
- All multiple-choice

The first math section is the Quantitative Reasoning section. On the Lower Level ISEE, this section has word problems. Some of the word problems require you to do calculations, but some do not. The problems that do not require you to do calculations are testing your ability to understand operations and interpret equations. There are 38 questions and you have 35 minutes to complete the section.

- Quantitative Reasoning has just word problems on Lower Level
- Not all problems require calculations
- 38 questions
- 35 minutes
- A little less than a minute per problem

The Mathematics Achievement section of the test is based on national standards for math. This means that it will look a little more like questions that you might be asked in school. All of the problems on the Mathematics Achievement section require calculations. There are 30 questions and you will have 30 minutes to complete the section. This means that you have a minute per problem.

- Mathematics Achievemt questions are based on national standards, which are probably very similar to your state standards
- All of the problems require calculations
- 30 questions
- 30 minutes
- One minute per question

So what is the difference between the two sections? On the Lower Level ISEE, not a whole lot. There are problems that could easily show up on either section. On the Middle and Upper Level ISEEs, there is a different problem type (quantitative comparisons) that shows up just on the quantitative reasoning section. However, quantitative comparisons are NOT on the Lower Level ISEE.

- On Lower Level, there are not huge differences between Quantitative Reasoning and Mathematics Achievement sections

Since the two quantitative sections are so similar, we will study them together.

Now- on to the strategies!

Quantitative Sections- Basic Strategies

On the quantitative sections, there are problems from a range of topics. The math is really not that hard. The ISEE is more about figuring out what they are asking and how to use the information given.

You will NOT be allowed to use a calculator on the ISEE. By using strategies, however, we can get to the right answers, often without using complicated calculations.

- No calculator allowed

The goal here is for you to get a general understanding of the key strategies for the math section. Following the basic strategies are content lessons where you will get to apply these new strategies.

Drumroll, please! The strategies are:

- Estimate- this is a multiple-choice test!
- If there are variables in the answer choices, try plugging in your own numbers
- If they ask for the value of a variable, plug in answer choices

Strategy #1: Estimate

You can spend a lot of time finding the exact right answer on this test, or you can spend time figuring out what answers couldn't possibly work and then choose from what is left.

For example, let's say the question is:

1. Use the pictures to the right to answer the question:

   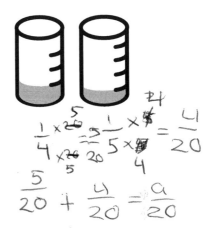

   The pictures show two jars that each hold 1 liter of liquid when they are full. They are not currently full (as shown). If the liquid from the two jars was combined, about how many liters of liquid would there be in total?

   (A) $\frac{9}{20}$ ✓
   (B) $1\frac{1}{5}$
   (C) $1\frac{1}{2}$
   (D) $2\frac{1}{4}$

We could read each jar and see that one jar has $\frac{1}{4}$ of a liter in it and the other jar has $\frac{1}{5}$ of a liter in it and then add those fractions together. However, we don't need to do that! We can clearly see that each jar is less than half full. That means that the total volume of the two combined would have to be less than a liter. Only answer choice A is less than a liter, so we can answer the question correctly without doing involved calculations.

You can use estimates on many of the problems, but in particular estimate when the question tells you to! You may see questions that ask for a "reasonable estimation" and then give answer choices in a range. Definitely estimate on those questions.

Some problems require you to use rounding. If you forget the rules for rounding, please read the following. If you remember the rules, just skip to the example problem.

Rules for Rounding

Is the number 78 closer to the number 70 or 80? If you said 80, you have a good idea of how rounding works. You have rounded 78 to the nearest 10, which is 80.

Now, what if you want to round a decimal number, like 3.43 to the nearest whole number? Would it be closer to 3 or to 4? The answer is that it is closer to 3. The special name for the "4" of the number 3.43 is the "rounding digit." Notice that when you round down, you drop the rounding digit and all the digits to its right.

Now that you see how rounding works, here are the rules:

- Round down if the rounding digit is 0, 1, 2, 3, or 4. This means to drop the rounding digit and all digits to its right.

For example, rounding 41.278543 to the nearest whole number means that the rounding digit is 2. Since 2 is less than 5, you will round down, meaning that you will drop the rounding digit 2 and all the numbers to its right. So 41.278543 will round to just plain 41.

- Round up if the rounding digit is 5, 6, 7, 8, or 9. This means to make the number to the left of the rounding digit one unit higher, and then drop the rounding digit and all the digits to its right.

For example, if we round the number 46.81 to the nearest whole number then the rounding digit is 8. It is five or greater, so you will round up. This means that the number 46.81 will be rounded up to 47.

Here are some other examples, with the rounding digit underlined:

Rounding to a whole number- The number 3.$\underline{5}$ is rounded up to 4.

Rounding to the nearest tenth- The number 2.7$\underline{3}$22, rounded to the nearest tenth, will be 2.7. Look at the rounding digit, which is 3, and you see that you will round down. So drop the rounding digit and all the digits to its right, and you are left with 2.7.

Here is an example of a question on the ISEE that requires you to use rounding:

1. Sean buys four items at the store that cost $3.21, $4.83, $6.05, and $2.99. What would be a reasonable estimate for the total cost of his items?
   (A) between $12 and $15
   (B) between $15 and $19 ✓
   (C) between $19 and $25
   (D) between $25 and $30

Without a calculator, finding the exact sum of the prices of the items would be kind of a bummer. However, the answer choices are just looking for a range, so we can round off. We would round off the prices to $3, $5, $6, and $3. If we add these numbers up, we get a total of $17. That clearly falls between $15 and $19, so answer choice B is correct.

Another way to use estimates is to come up with a range that the answer should fall within. You might just find that the answer choices are spread far enough apart that only one answer choice falls within your range. This is particularly helpful for subtractions problems with big numbers or problems that require subtracting fractions.

Here is an example where we can find a range:

1. Which is equal to the difference 3,000–245?
   (A) 2,555
   (B) 2,655
   (C) 2,755 ✓
   (D) 2,855

The first step to finding a range is to find a range for the number that is being subtracted. The number 245 is between 200 and 300. We subtract each of these numbers from 3,000 to get a range that the correct answer must fall in between.

$$3,000 - 200 = 2,800$$
$$3,000 - 300 = 2,700$$

We can see that the correct answer must be between 2,700 and 2,800. Only answer choice C falls between 2,700 and 2,800, so it is the correct answer.

Now that you know how to use estimates on the ISEE, be sure to complete the following practice drill to reinforce what you have learned. Practice using estimates on this drill, even if you know another way to solve.

Drill #1

1. Jack is making a juice cocktail. He combines $\frac{3}{4}$ cup of pineapple juice, $1\frac{1}{2}$ cup apple juice and $\frac{1}{3}$ cup of cranberry juice. How much total juice cocktail does he now have?
   (A) $1\frac{7}{8}$
   (B) $2\frac{7}{12}$
   (C) $3\frac{5}{12}$
   (D) $3\frac{7}{12}$

2. Carol did the following problem with her calculator.

   $$\frac{49 \times 592}{25}$$

   Which of the following would be a reasonable estimate for the answer that Carol's calculator showed?
   (A) between 900 and 1,300
   (B) between 1,300 and 1,500
   (C) between 1,500 and 1,800
   (D) between 1,800 and 2,100

3. Which is equal to the sum 203 + 396?
   (A) 579
   (B) 582
   (C) 589
   (D) 599

4. Which is equal to the value of the expression 4,000 − 275?
   (A) 3,525
   (B) 3,625
   (C) 3,725
   (D) 3,825

Drill #1

5. Jim buys five items. They cost $3.19, $0.99, $5.87, $7.00, and $2.49. Which is the best estimation of the total cost of Jim's items?
   (A) between $15 and $20 ✓
   (B) between $20 and $25
   (C) between $25 and $30
   (D) between $30 and $35

6. The area of the Gates of the Arctic National Park is about 11,756 square miles. Which National Park has an area that is closest to $\frac{2}{3}$ that of the Gates of the Arctic National Park?
   (A) Lake Clark National Park, which has an area of 4,093 square miles ✓
   (B) Glacier Bay National Park, which has an area of 5,038 square miles
   (C) Katmai National Park, which has an area of 5,761 square miles
   (D) Denali National Park, which has an area of 7,408 square miles

7. Which is equal to the sum 3.1 + 4.3 ?
   (A) $6\frac{9}{10}$
   (B) $7\frac{2}{5}$ ✓
   (C) $7\frac{9}{10}$
   (D) $8\frac{1}{2}$

8. In a grocery store, there are 21 aisles, each with 18 rows of shelves. Which expression would give the best estimate of the total number of shelves in the grocery store?
   (A) 20×10
   (B) 30×10
   (C) 20×20 ✓
   (D) 30×20

(Be sure to check your answers on p. 144)

Strategy #2: Plug in your own numbers if there are variables in the answer choices

What do I mean by variables in the answer choices? If you look at the answer choices and some or all of them have letters in addition to numbers, then you have variables in your answer choices.

- Look for letters in the answer choices

Here is how this strategy works:

1. Make up your own numbers for the variables.

    Just make sure they work within the problem. If they say that x is less than 1, do not make x equal to 2! If they say $x + y = 1$, then for heavens sake, don't make x equal to 2 and y equal to 3. Also, make sure that you write down what you are plugging in for your variables. EVERY TIME.

2. Solve the problem using your numbers.

    Write down the number that you get and circle it. This is the number you are trying to get with your answer choices when you plug in your value for the variable.

3. Plug the numbers that you assigned to the variables in step 1 into the answer choices and see which answer choice matches the number that you circled.

Here is an example:

1. Suzy has q more pencils than Jim. If Jim has 23 pencils, then how many pencils does Suzy have?

    (A) $q/23$

    (B) $q - 23$

    (C) $q + 23$ ✓

    (D) $23 - q$

Step 1: Plug in our own number.

Let's make q equal to 4. Suzy now has 4 more pencils than Jim.

Step 2: Solve using our own numbers.

If Jim has 23 pencils, and Suzy has four more than Jim, then Suzy must have 27 pencils. This is our target. Circle it. 27 is the number that we want to get when we plug in 4 for q in our answer choices.

Step 3: Plug into answer choices.

1. We are looking for the answer choice that would be equal to 27 when we plug in 4 for q.

   (A) $q/23 = 4/23$
   (B) $q - 23 = 4 - 23 = -19$
   (C) $q + 23 = 4 + 23 = 27$ ✓
   (D) $23 - q = 23 - 4 = 19$

Choice C gives us 27, which is what we were looking for, so we choose C and answer the question correctly.

There are not too many of this problem type on the ISEE. However, if you read through a problem and think, "this would be a lot easier if they gave us real numbers", then make up your own numbers! Sometimes the process of solving with real numbers will be enough to figure out what the correct answer is.

- If you think to yourself, "this problem would be a lot easier with real numbers", then plug in real numbers

Here is a practice drill to try out this new skill:

Drill #2

1. Sheila had *w* baseball cards. She gave five cards to Tommy but then she received three cards from Jill. In terms of *w*, how many cards did Sheila now have?
   (A) $w - 15$
   (B) $w - 8$
   (C) $w - 2$
   (D) $w + 2$

2. If the width of a rectangle is 4 times the length, *l*, which of the following gives the perimeter of the rectangle?
   (A) $3l$
   (B) $5l$
   (C) $10l$
   (D) $2(4 + l)$

3. Use the figure below to answer the question.

   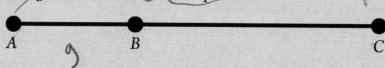

   The length of *AB* is *g* and the length of *AC* is *h*. What is the length of *BC*?
   (A) $h - g$
   (B) $h + g$
   (C) $g - h$
   (D) gh

4. If the perimeter of a rectangle is 18 in, which equation could be used to determine the length of that rectangle? ($P = 2l + 2w$, where $P =$ Perimeter, $l =$ length, and $w =$ width.)
   (A) $l = \frac{18 - w}{2}$
   (B) $l = \frac{18 - 2w}{2}$
   (C) $l = 18 - w$
   (D) $l = 2(18) - w$

   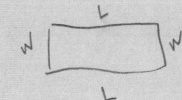

   $1L + 1L + W + W = 18$
   $2L + 2w = 18$
   $2L = 18 - 2w$
   $L = \frac{18 - 2w}{2}$

(Please check your answers on p. 144)

Strategy #3: If they ask for the value of a variable, plug in answer choices

On the ISEE, it is often easier to plug in answer choices and see what works. In particular, you may find this strategy most helpful on word problems. After all, this is a multiple-choice test so one of those answers has to work!

- Can often use this strategy on word problems
- This is a multiple-choice test

For this strategy, keep in mind that a variable is not always a letter. The problem might define x as the number of cars, or it might just ask you what the number of cars is. Either way, it is still asking for the value of a variable and you can use this strategy. The test writers might also thrown in a symbol, such as a small square, instead of a letter.

- A variable may not always be a letter, it can be any unknown quantity
- Sometimes there is a symbol, such as a small square, instead of a letter

Whenever a question asks for the value of a variable, whether it is a letter or something like the number of bunnies, one of those answer choices has to work. Since this is a multiple-choice test, you just have to figure out which one. Ruling out is one of our most important strategies and this scenario is just another example of how valuable a tool ruling out can be.

- Remember the mantra: Ruling out is good

Here is an example:

1. If three times a number is 18, what is the number?
   (A) 3
   (B) 6
   (C) 12
   (D) 15

To answer this question, we can simply plug in answer choices. If we plug in answer choice A and multiply 3×3, the answer is 9 and not 18. That tells us to rule out answer choice A. Now let's try out choice B. Since 6×3 does equal 18, answer choice B is correct.

For the following drill, try plugging in answer choices to see what works. Even if you know how to solve another way, you need to practice this strategy because there will be a time when you need it to bail you out.

1. Gertrude scored between 4 and 7 home runs in a softball game. When her brother asked her how many home runs she scored, she answered that she scored more than 5 home runs but less than 10. How many home runs did Gertrude score?
   (A) 5
   (B) 6
   (C) 7
   (D) 8

2. Which of the following could be the value of y in the equation $21 = 7y + 7$?
   (A) 2
   (B) 3
   (C) 4
   (D) 5

3. In the equation $3 \times (■ + 5) = 18$, what number could replace ■?
   (A) 1
   (B) 2
   (C) 3
   (D) 4

4. A pet store divided their mice into cages. If each cage had the same number of mice in it and there were 6 cages, which could be the total number of mice that the pet store has?
   (A) 11
   (B) 15
   (C) 21
   (D) 24

Drill #3

5. Sam is thinking of a number halfway between 15 and 21. What number is he thinking of?
   (A) 16
   (B) 17
   (C) 18
   (D) 19

6. If four times a number is 32, what is the number?
   (A) 4
   (B) 8
   (C) 12
   (D) 16

(Please check your answers on p. 144)

Those are the basic strategies that you need to know for the math section. As you go through the content sections, you will learn content and the strategies that work for specific problem types.

Answers to Math Strategies Drills

Drill #1

1. B
2. A
3. D
4. C
5. A
6. D
7. B
8. C

Drill #2

1. C
2. C
3. A
4. B

Drill #3

1. B
2. A
3. A
4. D
5. C
6. B

Math Content Sections

We have covered the basic strategies for the math sections. Now, we are going to take a look at some of the problem types that you will see on this test.

On the ISEE, sometimes the math to solve a problem is not that hard. However, the tough part of that problem might be recognizing what direction to go and what concept is being tested.

On the ISEE, there are six basic categories of math questions. They are:

- Whole numbers (integers)
- Fractions, decimals, and percents (which are basically fractions)
- Algebra (solving for variables)
- Probability and data analysis
- Geometry
- Measurement

The first four problem types listed above are the most likely to show up on the test. There are fewer of the geometry and measurement problems.

Doing well on the math sections is often a matter of decision-making. You need to decide what type of problem you are working on as well as what the most efficient way to solve will be.

Each lesson will:

- Teach you the facts that you need to know
- Show you how those facts are tested
- Give you plenty of practice

That is the book's side of the bargain, but you also have to keep up your end of the deal.

As you work through the content always ask yourself:

- What makes this problem unique?
- How will I recognize this problem in the future?

You are on your way to crushing the ISEE math section!

Whole Numbers on the ISEE

The first topic that we will cover is how whole numbers are tested on the ISEE.

In this section, we will cover:

- Different types of numbers
- How to write numbers in standard, expanded, and written forms
- Reading a number line
- Interpreting greater than/less than statements
- Basic operations
- Order of operations
- Properties (distributive, associative, commutative)
- Divisibility rules

Different types of numbers

On the ISEE, there are just a few types of numbers that you need to know.

They include:

- Integer/Whole number
- Positive/Negative
- Even/Odd
- Consecutive
- Prime/Composite

Integers and whole numbers are very similar. Simply put, they are numbers that do not have decimals or fractions. For example, 0, 1, 2, and 3 are all integers as well as whole numbers. The difference is that integers include negative numbers. On this test, however, they don't really require you to know the difference between integers and whole numbers. You just need to know that if they ask for an integer or a whole number, the correct answer cannot have a fraction or decimal.

- If they ask for an integer or whole number, no decimals or fractions

Positive numbers are those that are greater than zero. Negative numbers are those that are less than zero. The only tricky thing about positive and negative numbers is that zero is neither positive nor negative. The ISEE is not likely to ask you if zero is positive or negative, but they might tell you that a number must be positive, in which case you have to know that it can't equal zero.

- Zero is neither positive nor negative

Even numbers are those numbers that are evenly divisible by 2. That means that you can divide even numbers into groups of two with nothing left over. Odd numbers are those that cannot be evenly divided by 2. By this definition, zero is an even number because it can be divided by two with nothing left over. Even numbers are 0, 2 4 6, and so on. Odd numbers are 1, 3, 5, and so on.

- Zero is an even number

Consecutive numbers are simply integers that are next to each other when you count. For example, 1 and 2 are consecutive numbers. There are also consecutive even numbers and consecutive odd numbers. These are just the numbers that would be next to each other if you counted by twos. For example, 2 and 4 are consecutive even numbers and 1 and 3 are consecutive odd numbers.

- Consecutive just means in a row

Prime numbers are numbers greater than 1 that are only divisible by themselves and 1. For example, the number 7 is divisible only by itself and 1, so it is a prime number. A composite number is divisible by more than just itself and one. For example, the number six is divisible by 6, 1, 2, and 3, so it is a composite number. It is important to note that the only prime number that is even is 2. Also, the number 1 is neither prime nor composite.

- Prime numbers are only divisible themselves and 1
- Composite numbers are divisible by more than themselves and 1
- The only even prime number is 2
- The number 1 is neither prime nor composite

Here are some examples of questions that test these concepts:

1. On a piece of paper, Cheryl wrote down the following numbers: 2, 3, 5, 7. Which term best describes these numbers?
   (A) consecutive numbers
   (B) odd numbers
   (C) composite numbers
   (D) prime numbers

Let's use ruling out to solve this problem. Choice A might be tempting because the first two numbers in the sequence are consecutive. However, 3 and 5 are not consecutive numbers, so we can rule out choice A. We can also rule out choice B because 2 is included in the list of numbers and 2 is not an odd number. So now we just have to decide if the numbers are prime or composite. They are all only divisible by themselves and 1, so they are prime numbers. Choice D is correct.

2. Use the number set below to answer the question.

   (4, 6, 8, 10,....)

   Which of the following terms best describes the above set of numbers?
   (A) prime numbers
   (B) odd numbers
   (C) consecutive even numbers
   (D) negative numbers

If we look at choice A, it is clear that the numbers in the set are not prime, so we can rule out choice A. The numbers are also not odd, so choice B is out. We can also see that the numbers are not negative, so choice D can be ruled out. We are left with choice C- the correct answer.

How to write numbers in standard, expanded, and written forms

You may see a question on the ISEE that asks you to write a number in standard, expanded, or written form. The standard form of a number is simply how we normally write a number. For example, 492 is written in standard form. Expanded form breaks down a number by place value. For example, in expanded form, 492 would be 400 + 90 + 2. Written form just takes the expanded form and translates it into words. For example, 492 would become four hundred and ninety-two in written form.

In order to answer these questions, you have to know the basics of place value.

Here is a chart to help you remember place values. We will use the number 457,208 as an example.

400,000 +
50,000 +
7,000 +
200 +
8

4	5	7	2	0	8
Hundred thousands	Ten thousands	Thousands	Hundreds	Tens	Ones

Look at the digit 2, which is in the hundreds place. It represents a value of 200, because it represents 2 hundreds which is 200. Similarly, the digit 5 represents 5 ten thousands, so its value is 50,000.

The trick to this type of question is that you have to remember to mark place values that are not mentioned with zeroes. For example, let's say that a number is written out as "Four hundred thousand, thirty-two". When we write out this number, we have to start with putting a 4 in the hundred thousands place. However, we don't have any numbers to put in the ten thousands, thousands, and hundred places. We have to out zeroes in to mark these places. Then we put a 3 in the tens place to show the value of 30 and a 2 in the ones place. The final number in standard form is 400,032.

- Remember to mark empty place values with a zero

Here are some examples of how these concepts could be tested on the ISEE:

1. What is the standard form for nine hundred twenty-two thousand fifty-three?
   (A) 922,053
   (B) 900,253
   (C) 922,530
   (D) 920,253

To answer this question, let's think back to our place value chart. Let's fill in the information that is given in the question.

Hundred thousands	Ten thousands	Thousands	Hundreds	Tens	Ones
9	2	2		5	3

We can see that there was no value given for the hundreds place. That means that we must fill in a zero for that place value. Now our chart looks like this:

Hundred thousands	Ten thousands	Thousands	Hundreds	Tens	Ones
9	2	2	0	5	3

We can see that answer choice A is correct.

2. What statement correctly expresses the number 402,037?
   (A) four hundred twenty thousand thirty-seven
   (B) four hundred twenty thousand three hundred seven
   (C) four hundred two thousand three hundred seven
   (D) four hundred two thousand thirty-seven

Let's plug into our place value chart:

4	0	2	0	3	7
Hundred thousands	Ten thousands	Thousands	Hundreds	Tens	Ones

We can see that the written form should have four hundred and two thousand. This allows us to rule out choices A and B. We can also see that the 3 is in the tens place, so its value should be 30 and not 300. This allows us to rule out choice C. Choice D is correct.

3. What expression has the same value as 4,501?
   (A) 4,000 + 500 + 10 + 1
   (B) 4,000 + 500 + 1
   (C) 400 + 50 + 1
   (D) 1 + 400 + 5,000

This question is asking us to break down the number into expanded form. We can see that the 4 is in the 4 thousands place, so we know that the answer should have 4,000 in it. This allows us to rule out choices C and D since these answer choices put the 4 in the hundreds place. We can also see that there should not be any value in the tens place. This allows us to rule out choice A. Choice B is the correct answer.

Reading a number line

On the ISEE, you may have a question that asks you to read a number line. Generally, they give you a number line that has two points labeled and then ask you for the value of a third point. The key to answering these questions is to use the two points given to determine the scale, or what the number line is counting by. Is every dash on the line worth 1? Is it worth 2 (i.e. are they counting by twos)? Is each dash worth 5? That can be determined by looking at the two given points.

- Use the two given points to determine what the number line is counting by

Here are a couple of examples:

1. Use the figure below to answer the following question.

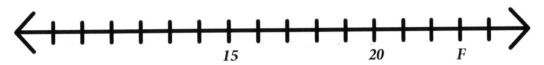

   Point *F* represents what number?
   (A) 19
   (B) 21
   (C) 23
   (D) 25

For this question, we need to use the 15 and the 20 to determine what the number line is counting by. The difference between 15 and 20 is five and there are five segments between the 15 and the 20 on the number line. That tells us that the number line is counting by 1. If we count up from the 20, we get that point *F* is equal to 23, so choice C is correct.

2. Use the figure below to answer the question.

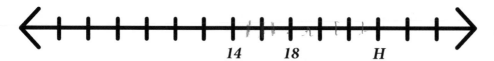

What number does point *H* represent on the number line?
(A) 16
(B) 20
(C) 21
(D) 24

Let's start by looking at the two numbers given. The numbers 14 and 18 are 4 numbers apart, but there are only two segments between them. That tells us that this number line is counting by 2s. If we count up from 18, we get that the next dash must be equal to 20, the dash after that must be equal to 22, and the dash that *H* represents must be equal to 24. Answer choice D is correct.

Interpreting greater than/less than statements

On the ISEE, you may see language that describes in words what you often see written with < or > signs.

You just have to translate these words into an inequality in order to solve.

Here is a cheat sheet for some of what you may see:

If they say:	Then it can be written as:
X is between 3 and 5	$3 < X < 5$ ✓
X is greater than 6	$X > 6$
X is less than 10	$X < 10$

The thing that you need to keep in mind about between, greater than, and less than is that they don't include the numbers themselves. For example, if X is between 3 and 5, then it cannot be either 3 or 5.

Here are a couple of examples of how these concepts are tested:

1. M is a whole number that is between 5 and 8. M is also between 6 and 13. Which of the following is M?

   (A) 5
   (B) 6
   (C) 7
   (D) 7.5

If we drew out a number line, we would see that our number has to be bigger than 6 and smaller than 8. That allows us to rule out choice A. Because the problem uses the word "between" we know that 6 cannot be included, so we can rule out choice B. That leaves us with choices C and D. However, the problem also says that M is a whole number. The number 7.5 is not a whole number, so choice D is out. Choice C is correct.

2. Caroline went on vacation for between 8 and 12 days. She was also on vacation for less than 10 days. How many days was Caroline on vacation?

   (A) 8
   (B) 9
   (C) 10
   (D) 11

From the first sentence of the question, we can rule out choice A. Since she was on vacation for "between 8 and 12 days", we know that the correct answer cannot be 8. From the second sentence of the question we know that she was on vacation for less than 10 days. That allows us to eliminate choices C and D since these numbers are not less than 10. Choice B is the correct answer.

Basic operations

There are two types of questions on the ISEE that test basic operations. There are some simple questions that just require you to do a calculation. Other questions are word problems that ask you to figure out what operation would be appropriate to fit the story given.

- Some questions just require a basic calculation
- Some questions are word problems that require you to figure out what operation should be performed

For problems that just ask you to perform a simple calculation, remember our strategy of estimating or finding a range.

- Remember to see if you can estimate or find a range before you perform the complete calculation

Here are a couple of examples of this type of problem:

1. What is the value of the sum 405 + 299?
   (A) 700
   (B) 704
   (C) 710
   (D) 714

To answer this question, let's first round off the second number. If we round 299 to the nearest hundred, we get 300. Now let's add 405 + 300. We get 705 as answer. Since we rounded up by one in the first step, let's take away one to get our final answer. If we take away 1, we are left with 704. Choice B is correct.

2. Which of the following is equal to the expression 4,000 − 235?
   (A) 3,765
   (B) 3,775
   (C) 3,785
   (D) 3,795

Let's use our strategy of finding a range for this one. The number 235 is between 230 and 240.

$$4,000 - 230 = 3,770$$
$$4,000 - 240 = 3,760$$

We now know that the correct answer must be between 3,770 and 3,760. Only answer choice A falls in that range, so choice A is correct.

Other questions will ask you to determine what operation to use. These questions are word problems.

Here is a quick guide for what operation to use when:

Operation	Situations where you would use that operation
Addition	• the question uses the word "sum" • you are given how many items are in different groups and asked for a total (each group does not have the same number of items in it)
Subtraction	• the question uses the word "difference" • you are given a total and the number of items in all but one of the groups and the question asks for that one group (each group does not have the same number of items in it)
Multiplication	• the question uses the word "product" • the question uses the word "of" • you are given how many groups there are and how many items are in each group and asked for a total (there are the same number of items in each group)
Division	• the question uses the word "quotient" • You are given a total and either the number of groups or the number of items in each group and asked for either the number of groups or the number of items in each group (there are the same number of items in each group)

Here are some examples of questions that test these concepts:

3. Fiona is creating a display at a store. She plans to stack cans in equal rows. Which equation would help her figure out how many total cans (c) she needs in order to create her display?
    (A) c = cans per row − number of rows
    (B) c = cans per row + number of rows
    (C) c = cans per row × number of rows
    (D) c = cans per row ÷ number of rows

For this problem, let's think about what situation we have in broader terms. We are looking for the total number of items that we need. That means that we would use either addition or multiplication. We also have groups (the rows) that all have the same number of items in them. That means that we should use multiplication. Answer choice C is correct.

4. Kevin took a poll of the 31 students in his class. He asked them whether they preferred to play soccer, baseball, or lacrosse. If 15 students said they preferred to play soccer and 7 students said that they preferred to play baseball, then how many students said they preferred to play lacrosse?
    (A) 9
    (B) 10
    (C) 16
    (D) 24

Let's take a close look at this situation. We are given the total number, so we know that we should be using subtraction or division. We are also given groups that do not have equal numbers, so we can narrow it down to subtraction. Now we have to do the actual calculations. We take the total and subtract the two groups that we are given: $31 - 15 - 7 = 9$. We know that there must be 9 students in the remaining group, so answer choice A is correct.

5. Mrs. Kline is trying to figure out how many goody bags she needs to make for a birthday party. She knows how many boys will be attending and how many girls will be attending. How could she figure out how many total goody bags (b) she will need?
    (A) b = number of girls × number of boys
    (B) b = number of girls + number of boys
    (C) b = number of girls − number of boys
    (D) b = number of girls ÷ number of boys

In this problem, we are looking for a total, so we know that we should use either addition or multiplication. We are not dealing with groups that are all the same size (we can't assume the groups are all the same size unless the problem states that), so we use addition. Answer choice B is correct.

6. Mr. Harris' class is going on a fieldtrip and needs to divide into groups of 5. If there are 35 students in Mr. Harris' class, then how many groups should they form?
    (A) 5
    (B) 6
    (C) 7
    (D) 8

This question gives us a total and then asks for the number of individual groups. Since the groups are all the same size, we use division: $35 \div 5 = 7$. Answer choice C is correct.

Order of operations

In school, you may have learned PEMDAS or Please Excuse My Dear Aunt Sally. These are both ways to remember the order of operations. Basically, the order of operations tells us which operations to do first when we are simplifying an expression.

We do anything in parentheses first (P), then exponents (E), then multiplication or division moving from left to right (MD), and finally addition or subtraction moving from left to right (AS).

For example, let's say we have the following expression:

$4 + (3 \times 5)$

We have to do what comes in parentheses first.

$4 + (15) = 19$

Notice that if we simply went from left to right, we would get a very different answer- and it would be wrong.

On the Lower Level ISEE, they won't test you on exponents. Generally, order of operations problems on the Lower Level are testing whether or not you recognize that the operation in parentheses must be done first.

Here are some examples for you to try:

1. What expression is equivalent to $3 \times (2+1)$?
   (A) $6 + 1$
   (B) 6×1
   (C) $3 + 3$
   (D) 3×3 ✓

For this question, we need to remember to do parentheses first. If we do $2 + 1$, then we get 3, so we replace the $2 + 1$ with a 3 and are left with 3×3, or answer choice D.

2. Use the equation below to answer the question.

$$\frac{10(25 + 50)}{5} = q$$

What is the value of q?
   (A) 75
   (B) 150
   (C) 300
   (D) 450

First, we have to do what is in the parentheses. This gives us:

$$\frac{10(75)}{5} = q$$

Our next step is to multiply the top (there are other ways to solve- this is just one of them):

$$\frac{750}{5} = q$$

If we divide 750 by 5, we get 150 for an answer, so answer choice B is correct.

3. Which of the following expressions has a value of 10?
   (A) $(2 \times 5) + 3 - 6$
   (B) $(2 \times 5 + 3) - 6$
   (C) $2 \times (5 + 3 - 6)$
   (D) $2 \times (5 + 3) - 6$

In order to answer this question, we need to solve each answer choice and see which one gives us 10 as an answer:

(A) $(2 \times 5) + 3 - 6 = 10 + 3 - 6 = 7$
(B) $(2 \times 5 + 3) - 6 = 13 - 6 = 7$
(C) $2 \times (5 + 3 - 6) = 2 \times 2 = 4$
(D) $2 \times (5 + 3) - 6 = 2 \times 8 - 6 = 16 - 6 = 10$

We can see that only answer choice D gives us 10 as an answer, so that is the correct answer choice.

Properties (distributive, associative, commutative)

On the Lower Level ISEE, there are three basic properties that might be tested.

The first (and most likely to be tested) is the distributive. Here is the general form for the distributive property:

$$A(B + C) = AB + AC$$
$$\text{or}$$
$$A(B - C) = AB - AC$$

You can remember this one because the number or variable in front is distributed (or handed out to) the numbers in parentheses. Notice that to use the distributive property we need to have either addition or subtraction within the parentheses.

The next property that you might be tested on is the associative property. The general form of the associative property is:

$$(A + B) + C = A + (B + C)$$
$$\text{or}$$
$$(A \times B) \times C = A \times (B \times C)$$

You can remember the associative property because the associations (or groups) change. Notice that this property works with addition and multiplication- it does not work with subtraction or division.

Finally, we have the commutative property. The general form of the commutative property is:

$$A + B + C = B + A + C$$
or
$$A \times B \times C = A \times C \times B$$

To remember this property, think about what commuting is. Commuting is getting from one place to another, and the commutative property moves numbers from one place to another. Notice that it only works with addition or multiplication- it does not work with subtraction or division.

Here are some examples of how these properties could be tested on the ISEE:

1. Which picture demonstrates the commutative property?
   (A) $\Delta + \nabla = \nabla + \Delta$
   (B) $\blacksquare(\nabla + \Delta) = \blacksquare\nabla + \blacksquare\Delta$
   (C) $\blacksquare(\nabla + \Delta) = \nabla(\Delta + \blacksquare)$
   (D) $(\blacksquare + \nabla) + \Delta = \blacksquare + (\nabla + \Delta)$

We are looking for the answer choice that gives us symbols that move around since we are looking for an example of the commutative property. Answer choice A is correct.

2. Which expression uses the distributive property correctly in order to solve $21 \times (2+7)$?
   (A) $(21 \times 2) + 7$
   (B) $2 \times (21 + 7)$
   (C) $7 \times (21 + 2)$
   (D) $(21 \times 2) + (21 \times 7)$

We are looking for the answer choice that distributes the 21 to both the 2 and the 7. Answer choice A just moves the parentheses, and would give us answer that wasn't even the same as the expression in the question. In answer choices B and C, the 21 is switched with another number. This is not even mathematically correct- we can only move numbers around if all the operations are addition or all the operations are multiplication. In answer choice D, the 21 is distributed to both the 2 and the 7, so it is the correct answer choice.

3. Which expression shows the associative property being used correctly?
   (A) $(X + Y) + Z = Z + (X + Y)$
   (B) $(X + Y) + Z = X + (Y + Z)$
   (C) $X + Y + Z = Z + Y + X$
   (D) $X(Y + Z) = XY + XZ$

With the associative property, groupings are changed. In answer choice A, the variables are moved around, but the groupings are not changed, so we can rule out choice A. In answer choice C, there are no groupings, so we can eliminate choice C as well. Choice D gets rid of the groupings (and shows the distributive property) but doesn't change the groupings, so it can be ruled out. Answer choice B shows the groupings change, and all the operations are addition, so it is the correct answer.

Divisibility rules

On the ISEE, it is helpful to know some basic divisibility rules. Could you do long division with every answer choice to see what is divisible by a certain number? Sure. Will it take you a long time to do this without a calculator? Yes.

Let's start with a basic definition. On the ISEE, you may see the words "divisible without a remainder". This simply means that we can divide one number by another with nothing left over. For example, if a number was divisible by 3, that means that you could divide that number by three and have nothing left over. Another way to say "divisible without a remainder" is "evenly divisible".

- "Divisible without a remainder" or "evenly divisible" just means that you can divide one number by another and have nothing left over

Here are some of the easier rules. There are rules for numbers divisible by 7 and 8, but they are really hard to remember and therefore not so helpful! The ISEE tends not to ask if large numbers are divisible by 7 or 8 anyway.

If …	Then it is divisible by…
the number is even	2
you add up all the digits of the number and the result is divisible by 3 (ex: 231 = 2 + 3 + 1 = 6 and 6 is divisible by 3)	3
the last two digits of your number are divisible by 4 (ex: 549624 and 24 is divisible by 4)	4
the number ends in 0 or 5	5
the number is divisible by both 2 and 3	6
you add up all the digits and the result is divisible by 9 (ex: 3726 = 3 + 7 + 2 + 6 = 18 and 18 is divisible by 9)	9
the number ends in 0	10

Here is a basic example of how divisibility could be tested:

1. Which of the following answer choices is divisible by 5?
    (A) 1,001
    (B) 1,002
    (C) 1,011
    (D) 1,015

To determine if a number is divisible by 5, we just look at the last digit. If the last digit is a zero or a five, then the whole number is divisible by 5. Only answer choice D has a last digit that is zero or five, so it is the correct answer choice.

2. Which answer choice is divisible by 6 without a remainder?
   (A) 824
   (B) 826
   (C) 828
   (D) 866

If a number is divisible by 6, it must be divisible by both 2 and 3. All of the answer choices are even, so they are all divisible by 2. Now, to see if the numbers are divisible by 3 we have to add up the digits and see if that number is divisible by 3.

(A) $8 + 2 + 4 = 14$- not divisible by 3

(B) $8 + 2 + 6 = 16$ - not divisible by 3

(C) $8 + 2 + 8 = 18$- IS divisible by 3

(D) $8 + 6 + 6 = 20$- not divisible by 3

Since only answer choice C is divisible by both 3 and 2, it is the only answer choice that is divisible by 6. Answer choice C is correct.

Some other questions don't use the word "divisible" at all! But they are still testing divisibility.

Here is an example:

3. If $t/4$ is a whole number, which of the following could be t?
   (A) 748
   (B) 758
   (C) 774
   (D) 802

In order for $t/4$ to be a whole number, t would have to be evenly divisible by 4. To figure out if a number is evenly divisible by 4, we look just at the last two digits. If we look at answer choice A, the last two digits are 48. 48 is divisible by 4, so choice A is correct.

An important rule to know is:

If a number is divisible by another number, then it is also divisible by the second number's factors.

Our rule for being divisible by 6 is based on this rule. The factors of 6 are 2 and 3. So if our number is divisible by both 2 and 3 (the factors of 6), then it is divisible by 6.

Here are a couple of examples of how this could be tested on the ISEE:

4. If w can be divided by both 3 and 7 without a remainder, then w could also be evenly divided by which other number?
   (A) 4
   (B) 11
   (C) 21
   (D) 28

Since w is divisible by both 3 and 7, it would also be divisible by a number that has 3 and 7 as factors. If we look at our answer choices, only choice C has 3 and 7 as factors. Choice C is correct.

5. Which number can be divided by 15 without leaving a remainder?
   (A) 1,010
   (B) 1,035
   (C) 1,045
   (D) 1,055

We don't have any divisibility rules for 15. However, factors of 15 are 3 and 5. This means that if the answer choice is divisible by BOTH 3 and 5, it will be divisible by 15. In order for a number to be divisible by 5, it must end in a 0 or a 5. All of our answer choice end in a 0 or a 5, though, so we can't use that to rule anything out. Now we have to see which answer choice is divisible by 3. In order to do that we add up the digits of each answer choice:

   (A) $1,010 = 1 + 0 + 1 + 0 = 2$, not divisible by 3
   (B) $1,035 = 1 + 0 + 3 + 5 = 9$, is divisible by 3
   (C) $1,045 = 1 + 0 + 4 + 5 = 10$, not divisible by 3
   (D) $1,055 = 1 + 0 + 5 + 5 = 11$, not divisible by 3

We can see that only choice B is divisible by 3 and 5, so it is the correct answer.

Those are the basics that you need to know about whole numbers on the ISEE. Be sure to complete the whole numbers practice set to reinforce what you have learned!

Whole numbers practice set

1. Noah wrote the following numbers on a piece of paper:
   $(4, 6, 8, 9, 10, \dots)$
   Which best describes the numbers that Noah wrote down?
   (A) even numbers
   (B) consecutive numbers
   (C) prime numbers
   (D) composite numbers

2. Use the number line below to answer the question.

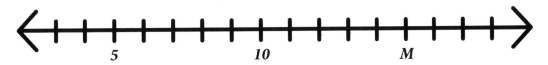

   What number does Point M represent on the number line?
   (A) 14
   (B) 15
   (C) 17
   (D) 20

3. Maria has to order t-shirts for all the players in her softball league. She knows how many players are in the league and she knows how many shirts come in a package. Which expression would she use to figure out how many packages (p) she should order?
   (A) $p =$ number of players ÷ number of shirts in a package
   (B) $p =$ number of players × number of shirts in a package
   (C) $p =$ number of shirts in a package − number of players
   (D) $p =$ number of shirts in a package ÷ number of players

4. Harold was thinking of a number that was greater than greater than 7 but less than 11. The number he was thinking of was also greater than 9 but less than 15. What number was Harold thinking of?
   (A) 8
   (B) 9
   (C) 10
   (D) 12

5. Which expression uses the distributive property correctly in order to solve $13 \times (9+2)$?
   (A) $(13 \times 9) + 2$
   (B) $(13 \times 9) + (13 \times 2)$
   (C) $9 \times (13 + 2)$
   (D) $2 \times (9 + 13)$

6. Which number can be divided by 9 with no remainder?
   (A) 2,088
   (B) 2,342
   (C) 2,409
   (D) 2,531

7. Which number shows the standard form for three hundred seventy thousand two hundred fourteen?
   (A) 307,214
   (B) 307,241
   (C) 370,204
   (D) 370,214

8. Which expression has a value of 16?
   (A) $(5 \times 7) - 4 + 1$
   (B) $5 \times (7 - 4 + 1)$
   (C) $5 \times (7 - 4) + 1$
   (D) $5 \times 7 - (4 + 1)$

9. When a number, y, is divided by both 4 and 5 there is no remainder. What other number could y be divided by with no remainder?
   (A) 9
   (B) 20
   (C) 25
   (D) 30

10. What is the value of the sum $512 + 302$?
   (A) 814
   (B) 834
   (C) 844
   (D) 852

Answers to the whole numbers practice set

1. D ✓
2. B ✓
3. A ✓
4. C ✗
5. B ✗
6. A ✓
7. D ✓
8. C ✓
9. B ✓
10. A ✓

Fractions, Decimals, and Percents

The fraction and decimal problems on the ISEE are pretty straightforward.

Here are some of the question types that you may see on the Lower Level ISEE:

- Determining a fraction from a picture
- Adding and subtracting fractions
- Multiplying and dividing with fractions
- Creating and using mixed numbers
- Comparing fractions
- Converting between fractions and decimals
- Adding and subtracting decimals
- Determining points on a number line using fractions and decimals
- Applying the basic concepts of percent

An important concept to remember throughout this section is that a fraction represents part out of a whole.

$$\text{Fraction} = \frac{\text{Part}}{\text{Whole}}$$

You also need to understand the basics of equivalent fractions.

The cardinal rule for equivalent fractions is that if you multiply (or divide) the top by some number, you must also multiply (or divide) the bottom by the same number in order for the value of the fraction to remain the same. This works when you multiply or divide the top and bottom by the same number. You can NOT add or subtract the same number from both the top and the bottom and keep the same value, however.

For example:

$$\frac{1}{2} \times \frac{2}{2} = \frac{2}{4}$$ Since we multiplied the numerator (top number) and denominator (bottom number) by the same number, we know that $\frac{1}{2} = \frac{2}{4}$

$$\frac{1}{2} + \frac{2}{2} = \frac{3}{4}$$ Since we added the same number to the numerator and denominator, $\frac{1}{4}$ is NOT equal to $\frac{3}{4}$

Determining a fraction from a picture

The first type of fraction problem that we will go over is how to tell what fraction of a picture is shaded.

The basic strategy for these problem types is that you need to divide your picture into pieces.

- Divide your pictures into pieces

This is easy if it is a figure that can be divided into equally sized pieces.

For example, if we have the following picture:

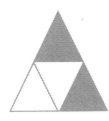

In this picture, we can see that there are four equally sized pieces. Two of those four pieces are shaded, so $1/2$ of the figure is shaded

Here is an example of how this could be tested on the ISEE:

1. In the hexagon to the right, what fraction of the hexagon is shaded?
   (A) $\frac{1}{2}$
   (B) $\frac{1}{3}$
   (C) $\frac{1}{4}$
   (D) $\frac{1}{6}$

In order to solve this problem, draw in lines that divide the hexagon into equal pieces.

It should look like this:

Now we can clearly see that one part out of six is shaded in, so the correct answer is choice D.

Sometimes you will have to divide a figure into unequal pieces to see what works. This question type always asks you to identify which figures have one half shaded in. It would be possible to write this question without using $1/2$ as the fraction that is shaded, but that would be a much harder problem type so the Lower Level ISEE is not likely to do that.

Here is an example of a figure that has one half shaded in but isn't easily divisible into pieces that are all the same size.

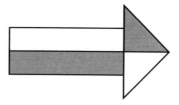

The key to these questions are just to match up parts that would be the same and then make sure that half of those parts are shaded.

Here is one for you to try:

2. Which of the following figures is NOT shaded in one half of its region?

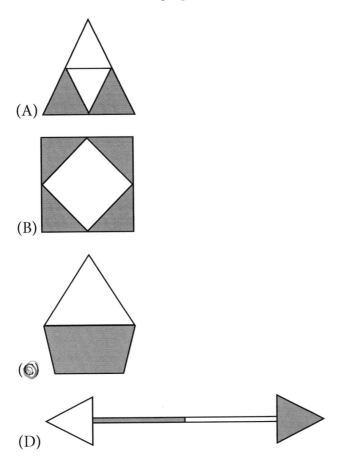

(A)

(B)

(C)

(D)

To answer this question, simply match up the shaded regions to identical non-shaded regions. If that doesn't work, then you have your correct answer. Choice C is the correct answer.

Another type of question on the ISEE that uses pictures is one that gives you a bunch of shapes and asks you what fraction of the shapes a certain shape is. These are easy- just count up the total number of shapes. This will be your denominator or bottom number. Then count up how many there are of the shape the questions asks for- this will be your numerator or top number. The only trick to these questions is that you often have to reduce the fraction in order to be able to choose the right answer choice.

- Add up total number of pictures- this is your denominator or bottom number
- Add up the number of pictures that are of the requested shape- this is your numerator or top number
- Remember to reduce if you can

Here are a couple of examples for you to try:

3. Kim drew these shapes on a piece of paper.

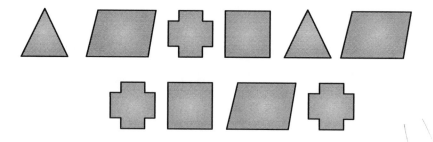

What fraction of the shapes are triangles?
(A) $\frac{1}{10}$
(B) $\frac{1}{5}$
(C) $\frac{3}{10}$
(D) $\frac{2}{5}$

Our first step is to count up the total number of shapes. There are 10 shapes so that becomes our denominator. Then we count up the number of triangles. There are 2 triangles so this our numerator. Our fraction now looks like this:

$$\frac{2}{10}$$

That is not an answer choice, however. We have to reduce the fraction in order to answer the question. We can see that 2 goes into both 2 and 10, so we will divide both the top and the bottom by 2.

$$\frac{2 \div 2}{10 \div 2} = \frac{1}{5}$$

Answer choice B is correct.

4. Use the pictures below to answer the question.

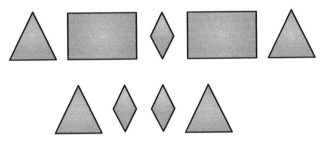

What fraction of the pictures are kites?
(A) $\frac{2}{9}$
(B) $\frac{1}{4}$
(C) $\frac{1}{3}$
(D) $\frac{1}{2}$

First, we count up the total number of shapes. There are 9 total shapes, so that is our denominator. Of these shapes, three are kites- that will be our numerator. Now we have to reduce.

$$\frac{3}{9} = \frac{3 \div 3}{9 \div 3} = \frac{1}{3}$$

We can see that answer choice C is correct.

Adding and subtracting fractions

We use equivalent fractions to get the same bottom number, also known as a common denominator. We then add (or subtract) across the top and keep the common denominator as the denominator in our answer.

For example:

Let's say our problem looks like this:

$$\frac{1}{2} + \frac{2}{3} = ?$$

$\frac{1}{2} \times \frac{3}{3} = \frac{3}{6}$

$\frac{2}{3} \times \frac{2}{2} = \frac{4}{6}$

$\frac{3}{6} + \frac{4}{6} = \frac{7}{6}$

We are looking for a number that both denominators go into, or are factors of. 2 and 3 both go into 6, so 6 will be our common denominator.

$$\frac{1}{2} \times \frac{3}{3} = \frac{3}{6}$$

We use equivalent fractions to get a common denominator

$$\frac{2}{3} \times \frac{2}{2} = \frac{4}{6}$$

We can now add the equivalent fractions:

$$\frac{3}{6} + \frac{4}{6} = \frac{7}{6}$$ We add across the top but keep the common denominator

We aren't quite done yet. We now have a fraction where the top number is bigger than the bottom number (an improper fraction). To fix this, we can break apart the fraction.

$$\frac{7}{6} = \frac{6}{6} + \frac{1}{6}$$ We break the fraction apart so that we can see how many "ones" we have and what fraction is left.

Finally, we can create a mixed number as an answer.

$$\frac{6}{6} + \frac{1}{6} = 1 + \frac{1}{6} = 1\frac{1}{6}$$

Here are a couple of examples of basic addition and subtraction questions:

1. What is the value of the expression $\frac{1}{3} + \frac{2}{5}$?
    (A) $\frac{1}{3}$
    (B) $\frac{3}{5}$
    (C) $\frac{11}{15}$
    (D) $\frac{4}{5}$

$$\frac{5}{15} + \frac{6}{15} = \frac{11}{15}$$

To answer this question, we first have to get a common denominator. The smallest number that both 3 and 5 go into is 15. This means that 15 will be our common denominator. Now we have to use the principles of equivalent fractions.

$$\frac{1}{3} \times \frac{5}{5} = \frac{5}{15}$$

$$\frac{2}{5} \times \frac{3}{3} = \frac{6}{15}$$

Now we just have to add the fractions with common denominators together.

$$\frac{5}{15} + \frac{6}{15} = \frac{11}{15}$$

We can see that answer choice C is correct.

2. What is the value of the expression $\frac{3}{4} - \frac{2}{3}$?
    (A) $\frac{1}{12}$
   (B) $\frac{1}{6}$
   (C) $\frac{1}{3}$
   (D) $\frac{1}{2}$

To answer this question, we first need to create a common denominator.

$$\frac{3 \times 3}{4 \times 3} = \frac{9}{12}$$

$$\frac{2 \times 4}{3 \times 4} = \frac{8}{12}$$

Now we can do the actual subtraction.

$$\frac{9}{12} - \frac{8}{12} = \frac{1}{12}$$

We can see that answer choice A is the correct answer choice.

You may very well also see word problems that require you to apply these concepts.

Here are some examples for you to try:

3. Katie has two jars of mayonnaise. One jar has $\frac{1}{4}$ cup of mayonnaise left in it and the other jar has $\frac{2}{5}$ cup of mayonnaise left in it. How many total cups of mayonnaise does Katie have?
   (A) $\frac{1}{3}$
   (B) $\frac{1}{2}$
   (C) $\frac{13}{20}$
   (D) $\frac{3}{5}$

First, we need to figure out what operation to use. We are given two parts and asked for the total, so we use addition. In order to add two fractions, we have to first find the common denominator.

$$\frac{1 \times 5}{4 \times 5} = \frac{5}{20}$$

$$\frac{2 \times 4}{5 \times 4} = \frac{8}{20}$$

Now we add the two fractions with common denominators together.

$$\frac{5}{20} + \frac{8}{20} = \frac{13}{20}$$

We can see that answer choice C is correct.

4. Taylor had $2\frac{1}{2}$ cups of sugar. She gave $\frac{3}{4}$ cup of sugar to her neighbor. How much sugar did Taylor have left?
   (A) $1\frac{1}{2}$
   (B) $1\frac{3}{4}$
   (C) 2
   (D) $2\frac{1}{4}$

To answer this question, we first have to decide what operation to use. Since Taylor is giving away some sugar, we use subtraction. To do subtraction, we have to have a common denominator.

$$2\frac{1}{2} = 2\frac{1 \times 2}{2 \times 2} = 2\frac{2}{4}$$

Now our problem looks like this:

$$2\frac{2}{4} - \frac{3}{4}$$

Our issue now is that we can't subtract $\frac{3}{4}$ from $\frac{2}{4}$. We will have to borrow from the 2.

$$2\frac{2}{4} = 1 + 1 + \frac{2}{4} = 1 + \frac{4}{4} + \frac{2}{4} = 1\frac{6}{4}$$

We now have an improper fraction with a numerator that is bigger than the denominator. This is what we need in order to do the subtraction problem.

$$1\frac{6}{4} - \frac{3}{4} = 1\frac{3}{4}$$

We can see that the correct answer is choice B.

Multiplying and dividing with fractions

On the Lower Level ISEE, multiplying and dividing with fractions will be tested primarily with word problems.

In general, to multiply fractions, we simply multiply across the top and multiply across the bottom.

For example:

$$\frac{1}{2} \times \frac{2}{3} = \frac{2}{6}$$

We then have to reduce the fraction since there is a number that goes into both the numerator and denominator. We use our rule of equivalent fractions (do the same to the top and bottom), only this time we are dividing.

$$\frac{2 \div 2}{6 \div 2} = \frac{1}{3}$$

Our final answer would be $\frac{1}{3}$.

Those really are the basics for what you need to know about fractions. That's not so bad, right?

Now let's move on to how these basics will be tested.

On the ISEE, you will more commonly be asked to multiply a fraction by a whole number. To do this, we just put the whole number over one.

Here is an example:

$$450 \times \frac{1}{3} = \frac{450}{1} \times \frac{1}{3} = \frac{450}{3}$$

For our next step, we have to understand that a fraction bar essentially means to divide.

$$\frac{450}{3} = 450 \div 3 = 150$$

To divide fractions, we flip the second fraction and then multiply.

For example, let's say our problem was:

$$\frac{2}{3} \div \frac{4}{5}$$

In order to find our answer, we flip the second fraction and multiply, so our problem becomes:

$$\frac{2}{3} \times \frac{5}{4} = \frac{2 \times 5}{3 \times 4} = \frac{10}{12}$$

We aren't quite done yet since we still have to reduce. Because 10 and 12 are both divisible by 2, we divide the top and the bottom by 2.

$$\frac{10 \div 2}{12 \div 2} = \frac{5}{6}$$

Our final answer is $5/6$.

If we have division with a fraction and a whole number, we have to remember to put the whole number over 1.

For example, let's say that we want to divide $\frac{1}{3}$ into 3 parts. The math would look like this:

$$\frac{1}{3} \div 3 = \frac{1}{3} \div \frac{3}{1} = \frac{1}{3} \times \frac{1}{3} = \frac{1}{9}$$

On the ISEE, you will most likely see word problems that test multiplication and division of fractions.

Here are some for you to try:

1. Lee has $\frac{3}{4}$ gallon of chocolate milk. He wants to divide it evenly among four cups. How much chocolate milk should go in each cup?
   (A) $\frac{3}{16}$ gallon
   (B) $\frac{1}{4}$ gallon
   (C) $\frac{1}{3}$ gallon
   (D) $\frac{2}{3}$ gallon

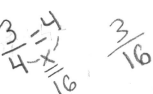

Since the problem uses the word divide, we know that division is in order. We have to divide $\frac{3}{4}$ into 4 parts, so we $\frac{3}{4} \div 4$. The math would look like this:

$$\frac{3}{4} \div 4 = \frac{3}{4} \div \frac{4}{1} = \frac{3}{4} \times \frac{1}{4} = \frac{3}{16}$$

Answer choice A is correct.

2. The distance from Chicago to Los Angeles is roughly 2,015 miles. Marni is driving from Chicago to Los Angeles and wants to stay overnight when she has driven about $\frac{1}{4}$ of the distance from Chicago to Los Angeles. Where should she stay?
   (A) Des Moines, Iowa, which is 332 miles from Chicago
   (B) Lincoln, Nebraska, which is 522 miles from Chicago
   (C) Denver, Colorado, which is 1,004 miles from Chicago
   (D) Las Vegas, Nevada, which is 1,751 miles from Chicago

In order to find the distance, we need to find $\frac{1}{4}$ of 2,015 miles. The word "of" tells us that we should multiply.

$$2,015 \times \frac{1}{4} = \frac{2,015}{1} \times \frac{1}{4} = \frac{2,015}{4}$$

From here, we can estimate since this is a multiple-choice test. 2,015 is about 2,000.

$$\frac{2,000}{4} = 500$$

We are looking for the answer choice that is close to 500 miles. Answer choice B comes the closest.

Creating and using mixed numbers

Mixed numbers are numbers that have a whole number part and a fraction part.

For example, $2\frac{1}{2}$ is a mixed number. Mixed numbers can also be converted into improper fractions, or fractions where the top number is larger than the bottom number.

On the ISEE, the numbers that you have to convert generally are not that big. There are multiple methods to convert between mixed numbers and improper fractions, but we will show you just one that works well with smaller numbers.

Let's say we want to change $2\frac{1}{2}$ into an improper fraction. We can start by breaking down the whole number into ones.

$$2\frac{1}{2} = 1 + 1 + \frac{1}{2}$$

Our next step is to convert the ones into fractions that have the same denominator as the fraction in the mixed number.

$$2\frac{1}{2} = 1 + 1 + \frac{1}{2} = \frac{2}{2} + \frac{2}{2} + \frac{1}{2}$$

Now we just add the fractions together.

$$\frac{2}{2} + \frac{2}{2} + \frac{1}{2} = \frac{5}{2}$$

We are left with the improper fraction $\frac{5}{2}$ that is equal to the mixed number $2\frac{1}{2}$.

We can use the same process, only in reverse, to turn an improper fraction into a mixed number.

For example, let's say we want to convert $\frac{11}{4}$ into a mixed number.

First, we have to break down $\frac{11}{4}$.

$$\frac{11}{4} = \frac{4}{4} + \frac{4}{4} + \frac{3}{4}$$

Now we just turn the $\frac{4}{4}$s into ones.

$$\frac{4}{4} + \frac{4}{4} + \frac{3}{4} = 1 + 1 + \frac{3}{4} = 2\frac{3}{4}$$

We now know that $\frac{11}{4}$ is equal to $2\frac{3}{4}$.

On the ISEE, these concepts are often tested as word problems.

Here are some examples for you to try:

1. Paul is putting together bags of mixed nuts. He combined the nuts in the recipe below and then divided the nuts equally into 6 bags.

   MIXED NUTS
   8 cups peanuts
   4 cups brazil nuts
   3 cups cashews
   5 cups walnuts

   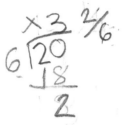

   About how many cups of nuts were in each bag?
   (A) $2\frac{1}{2}$
   (B) $2\frac{2}{3}$
   (C) $3\frac{1}{6}$
   (D) $3\frac{1}{3}$

To answer this question, first we have to figure out how many total cups of nuts we are dividing. If we add up the amounts from the recipe ($8 + 4 + 3 + 5 = 20$), we find that there are a total of twenty cups of nuts. Now we have to divide the total (20) by the number of bags (6) in order to figure out how many cups of nuts are in each bag.

$$\frac{20}{6} = \frac{6}{6} + \frac{6}{6} + \frac{6}{6} + \frac{2}{6} = 1+1+1+ \frac{2}{6} = 3\frac{1}{3}$$

Answer choice D is correct.

2. Nora is making fruit punch. She combines $2\frac{1}{2}$ cups pineapple juice with $3\frac{3}{4}$ cups cranberry juice. How many cups of fruit punch will she have?
   (A) $5\frac{3}{4}$
   (B) $6\frac{1}{4}$
   (C) $6\frac{1}{2}$
   (D) $6\frac{3}{4}$

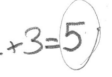

In order to answer this question, we first have to get a common denominator for the fractions. Both 2 and 4 go into 4, so we will make that our common denominator. The number $3\frac{3}{4}$ already has a denominator of 4, so we can leave that number alone. We need to convert $2\frac{1}{2}$, however.

$$2\frac{1}{2}=2\frac{1\times 2}{2\times 2}=2\frac{2}{4}$$

Now we break apart our mixed numbers and use the commutative property to group the whole numbers and the fractions.

$$2\frac{2}{4}+3\frac{3}{4}=2+\frac{2}{4}+3+\frac{3}{4}=2+3+\frac{2}{4}+\frac{3}{4}=5+\frac{5}{4}=5\frac{5}{4}$$

Our problem now is that the fraction part of our mixed number needs to be reduced.

$$5\frac{5}{4}=5+\frac{4}{4}+\frac{1}{4}=5+1+\frac{1}{4}=6\frac{1}{4}$$

Answer choice B is correct.

Sometimes, when we are subtracting mixed numbers, we need to borrow in order to subtract.

For example, let's say we have the following problem:

$$3\frac{1}{3}-\frac{2}{3}=$$

The issue here is that we cannot take $\frac{2}{3}$ away from $\frac{1}{3}$. We have to borrow from the 3.

$$3\frac{1}{3}=1+1+1+\frac{1}{3}=1+1+\frac{3}{3}+\frac{1}{3}=2\frac{4}{3}$$

Now we can subtract.

$$2\frac{4}{3}-\frac{2}{3}=2\frac{2}{3}$$

By borrowing we can find that $3\frac{1}{3}-\frac{2}{3}$ is equal to $2\frac{2}{3}$.

Here are a couple of questions for you to try:

3. Peter had $3\frac{1}{4}$ feet of rope. He gave Tom $1\frac{3}{4}$ feet of that rope. How many feet of rope did Peter have left?

(A) $1\frac{1}{2}$
(B) $2\frac{1}{4}$
(C) $2\frac{1}{2}$
(D) $3\frac{1}{4}$

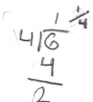

In order to answer this question, we have to subtract $1\frac{3}{4}$ from $3\frac{1}{4}$. In order to do this, we have to borrow a 1 from the 3 in the first fraction.

$$3\frac{1}{4} = 2 + 1 + \frac{1}{4} = 2 + \frac{4}{4} + \frac{1}{4} = 2\frac{5}{4}$$

We can now do the subtraction problem.

$$2\frac{5}{4} - 1\frac{3}{4} = 1\frac{2}{4}$$

Now we just have to reduce the $\frac{2}{4}$.

$$1\frac{2}{4} = 1\frac{2 \div 2}{4 \div 2} = 1\frac{1}{2}$$

The correct answer is choice A.

4. Steve had $4\frac{1}{2}$ cups of sugar. He used some of that sugar in a recipe. He now has $2\frac{7}{8}$ cups of sugar left. How many cups of sugar did he use in his recipe?

(A) $\frac{1}{2}$
(B) $\frac{5}{8}$
(C) $1\frac{3}{8}$
(D) $1\frac{5}{8}$

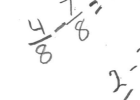

In order to find how much sugar we used, we have to subtract how much sugar Steve had left from how much sugar he started with.

$$4\frac{1}{2} - 2\frac{7}{8}$$

We need to borrow from the 4 and then get a common denominator.

$$4\frac{1}{2}=4+\frac{1}{2}=3+1+\frac{1}{2}=3+\frac{2}{2}+\frac{1}{2}=3\frac{3}{2}=3\frac{3\times4}{2\times4}=3\frac{12}{8}$$

Now we can subtract.

$$3\frac{12}{8}-2\frac{7}{8}=1\frac{5}{8}$$

Answer choice D is correct.

Comparing fractions

There are all sorts of ways to compare fractions. On the Lower Level ISEE, however, you generally just have to be able to compare fractions to one-half. They generally don't phrase the question as asking whether or not a fraction is greater than or less than one-half, however. They might ask which fraction is greatest and three of the four answer choices are less than one-half. They might ask if a fraction is between one-half and a larger fraction, but three of the answer choices are less than one-half.

- On comparing fraction questions, you can almost always use $\frac{1}{2}$ as a comparison point- remember that this is a multiple-choice test!

To use one-half as a comparison point, we often have to create a fraction that is equivalent to one-half. This fraction should have the same numerator as the fraction we are comparing to one-half.

For example, let's say we want to know if $\frac{8}{15}$ is greater or less than $\frac{1}{2}$.

Fraction for comparison	Fraction equal to $\frac{1}{2}$	Which is bigger?
$\frac{8}{15}$	$\frac{1\times8}{2\times8}=\frac{8}{16}$	$\frac{8}{15}$

The trick to this comparison is to remember that as the bottom number (denominator) gets bigger, the fraction actually gets smaller if the top number (numerator) stays the same.

- Create a fraction that is equal to $\frac{1}{2}$ and has the same numerator as the fraction you are comparing it to

- If two fractions have the same numerator, then the fraction with the larger denominator actually has a lower overall value

Here are a couple of questions for you to try:

1. Which fraction is smallest?
   (A) $\frac{4}{7}$
   (B) $\frac{6}{11}$
   (C) $\frac{7}{15}$
   (D) $\frac{10}{19}$

To answer this question, let's make a chart to compare each number to one-half:

Answer Choice	Fraction equal to $\frac{1}{2}$	Which is bigger?
(A) $\frac{4}{7}$	$\frac{4}{8}$	Answer choice
(B) $\frac{6}{11}$	$\frac{6}{12}$	Answer choice
(C) $\frac{7}{15}$	$\frac{7}{14}$	$\frac{1}{2}$
(D) $\frac{10}{19}$	$\frac{10}{20}$	Answer choice

From this chart we can see that the only answer choice that is less than one-half is answer choice C. Answer choice C is correct.

2. Which fraction is between $\frac{2}{9}$ and $\frac{1}{2}$?

   (A) $\frac{3}{7}$

   (B) $\frac{4}{7}$

   (C) $\frac{5}{9}$

   (D) $\frac{7}{9}$

Any fraction that is between $\frac{2}{9}$ and $\frac{1}{2}$ must be less than $\frac{1}{2}$, so we should compare each answer choice to $\frac{1}{2}$. If we do this, the odds are good that we will only have one potential correct answer.

Answer Choice	Fraction equal to $\frac{1}{2}$	Which is bigger?
(A) $\frac{3}{7}$	$\frac{3}{6}$	$\frac{1}{2}$
(B) $\frac{4}{7}$	$\frac{4}{8}$	Answer choice
(C) $\frac{5}{9}$	$\frac{5}{10}$	Answer choice
(D) $\frac{7}{9}$	$\frac{7}{14}$	Answer choice

Since answer choice A is the only answer choice that is less than $\frac{1}{2}$, we don't even have to worry about whether it is greater than $\frac{2}{9}$. Answer choice A is correct.

Converting between fractions and decimals

On the Lower Level ISEE, questions that ask you to convert from a fraction to a decimal are really just testing your understanding of place value.

For example, if we have three tenths (written as 0.3), then another way to write the value of that decimal is $\frac{3}{10}$. If we have 0.04, then that is equal to four hundredths or $\frac{4}{100}$.

Here are a couple of questions for you to try:

1. Which fraction has the same value as 0.9

   (A) $\frac{1}{9}$

   (B) $\frac{1}{90}$

   (C) $\frac{9}{10}$

   (D) $\frac{9}{100}$

In the decimal 0.9, the 9 has the value of nine-tenths. Answer choice C correctly shows this relationship.

2. Which decimal is equivalent to $\frac{5}{100}$?
   (A) 5.0
   (B) 0.5
   (C) 0.05
   (D) 0.005

If we think back to our place value chart, we know that the hundredths place is two spots to the right of the decimal point. We put the decimal point, then we put a zero to mark the empty tenths place, and then we put the 5 in the hundredths place. Answer choice C is correct.

Adding and subtracting decimals

You won't have to do complicated decimal calculations on the Lower Level ISEE. You will need to know how to add and subtract decimals, however. The key is just to remember to line up the decimal points.

- To add or subtract decimals, just line up the decimal points

For example, let's say we want to add 3.5 and 2.6. The math would look like this:

```
  3.5
+2.6
-----
  6.1
```

When you have a decimal point, just remember to carry over and borrow just like you would with normal addition and subtraction.

- Remember to carry and borrow, just like any other addition/subtraction problem

Here is a basic question for you to answer:

1. Which is equal to 6.7 − 5.3?
   (A) 1.2
   (B) 1.4
   (C) 1.9
   (D) 2.4

If we first take away 3 tenths from 7 tenths, you can see that the decimal portion of our answer should be 4 tenths, so answer choice B or answer choice D must be correct. If we subtract 5 from 6, we can see that we would have a 1 left over in the units place. If we put the decimal portion together with the units portion, we can see that 1.4, or answer choice B, is correct.

More often, decimal questions will ask you to combine several skills. You may have to find the answer as a decimal, and then convert that decimal to a fraction, and finally reduce that fraction.

Here are a couple of sample questions for you to try:

2. Which is equal to 3.8 + 2.6?
   (A) $5\frac{3}{4}$
   (B) 6
   (C) $6\frac{1}{10}$
   (D) $6\frac{2}{5}$

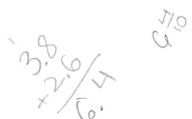

Our first step is to add together 3.8 and 2.6. If we do that, we can see that 3.8 + 2.6 is equal to 6.4. Our answers are given as mixed numbers, however. We need to convert 6.4 into a mixed number. We can leave the 6 part alone, we just need to write the 0.4 part as a fraction. If we think of 0.4 as being equal to 4 tenths, then it is easy to convert into a fraction and reduce.

$$6.4 = 6\frac{4}{10} = 6\frac{4 \div 2}{10 \div 2} = 6\frac{2}{5}$$

Answer choice D is correct.

3. Which is equal to 4.2 - 2.9?
   (A) $1\frac{3}{10}$
   (B) $1\frac{1}{3}$
   (C) $2\frac{1}{10}$
   (D) $2\frac{7}{10}$

First we need to do the subtraction problem to find a decimal answer. If we subtract 2.9 from 4.2, we get 1.3 as an answer. The 1 in the units places tells us that our answer should start with a 1. We then have to convert the 0.3 part of our answer into a fraction. Since the 3 is in the tenths place, we put 3 over ten to create $\frac{3}{10}$. If we add the 1 in the units place, we can see that our answer is $1\frac{3}{10}$, or answer choice A.

Finally, you may see a word problem that requires you to apply the rules of decimals.

Here is an example for you to try:

4. Carl went shopping and bought four items. He bought a candy bar that cost $1.25, a sandwich that cost $4.50, an apple that cost $0.75, and a bottle of juice. If he spent a total of $8.25, how much did the bottle of juice cost?
    (A) $1.50
    (B) $1.75
    (C) $2.00
    (D) $2.25

Our first step in answering this question is to add up the value of the items that we do know the costs of.

$1.25 + $4.50 + $0.75 = $6.50

Now we have to subtract the total of the items that we know ($6.50) from the total amount of money that Carl spent.

$8.25 − $6.50 = $1.75

We can see that answer choice B is correct.

Determining points on a number line using fractions and decimals

You may see questions on the Lower Level ISEE that require you to assign fraction or decimal values to points on a number line. Just like other number line problems, the key is to figure out what the number line is counting by. They will give you two identified points and you need to use those points to figure out how much each segment between dashes is worth.

- Use the two points given to determine what the number line is counting by

Here are a couple of examples of number line problems that require you to use fractions and decimals.

1. Use the number line below to answer the question.

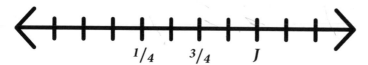

What value does point J represent?

(A) $\frac{1}{2}$

(B) 1

(C) $1\frac{1}{4}$

(D) $1\frac{1}{2}$

First we need to see what the number line is counting by. We can see that there is one dash between $\frac{1}{4}$ and $\frac{3}{4}$. The fraction $\frac{2}{4}$ (or $\frac{1}{2}$ if we reduce) falls right in between $\frac{1}{4}$ and $\frac{3}{4}$, so we know that the number line is counting by $\frac{1}{4}$. Now we need to count up by $\frac{1}{4}$ until we get to point J. The dash after the $\frac{3}{4}$ dash would be $\frac{4}{4}$, which reduces to one. The dash after that (or point J) would therefore represent $1\frac{1}{4}$. Answer choice C is correct.

2. Use the number line below to answer the question.

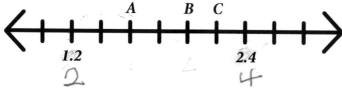

Which three numbers do points A, B, and C represent?

(A) 1.3, 1.5, 1.6

(B) 1.4, 1.6, 1.7

(C) 1.6, 1.8, 2.0

(D) 1.6, 2.0, 2.2

To answer this question, we have to figure out what the number line is counting by. There are six segments between 1.2 and 2.4. If we find the difference between 2.4 and 1.2, we can see that the six segments cover 1.2 units. This means that each segment must be equal to 0.2. We are counting by 0.2. This means that the first dash to the right of 1.2 would be 1.4, and the following dash (point A) would be 1.6. If we keep counting by 0.2, we get that point B is equal to 2.0 and point C is equal to 2.2. Answer choice D is correct.

Applying the basic concepts of percent

On the Lower Level ISEE, there will not be super hard questions requiring you to calculate percents. You may need to understand the basic concept, however.

A percent is simply a fraction that has 100 as its denominator. What percents essentially do is give us a common denominator of 100 so that we can easily compare numbers.

Let's look at an example. Let's say we polled 10 students about their favorite class. If all of the students said that math class was their favorite, then 100% of the students liked math class the most. If no students said that grammar class was their favorite class, then 0% chose grammar class. If 5 students said that their favorite class was science, then 50% of the students chose science.

Here are some examples that test these basic concepts:

1. Out of the 28 students in Mr. Kline's class, none of them remembered to return his or her permission slip. What percent of students returned a permission slip?
   (A) 0%
   (B) 25%
   (C) 50%
   (D) 100%

Since zero students out of 28 returned a permission slip, the percent would be 0%. Answer choice A is correct.

2. There are 75 second graders in Happy Hills school. If they are all going on a fieldtrip, what percent of the second graders are going on a fieldtrip?
   (A) 0%
   (B) 25%
   (C) 75%
   (D) 100%

The word "all" tells us that 75 out of 75 students are going on a fieldtrip. The word "all" is also a signal that 100% of the students are going. Answer choice D is correct.

3. If half of the students in Ms. Harris' class are boys, what percent of the students in Ms. Harris' class are boys?
   (A) 0%
   (B) 25%
   (C) 50%
   (D) 75%

Let's convert the word "half" into a fraction. We would write this as $\frac{1}{2}$. Now we just need to find an equivalent fraction for $\frac{1}{2}$ that has 100 as the denominator.

$$\frac{1}{2} = \frac{1 \times 50}{2 \times 50} = \frac{50}{100} = 50\%$$

Answer choice C is correct.

Those are the basics that you need to know about fractions, decimals, and percents for the Lower Level ISEE. Be sure to complete the fractions, decimals, and percents practice set to practice what you have learned.

Fractions, decimals, and percents practice set

1. Which fraction is the largest?
    (A) $\frac{6}{11}$
    (B) $\frac{7}{15}$
    (C) $\frac{8}{19}$
    (D) $\frac{9}{19}$

2. Use the pictures below to answer the question.

    The two containers above each hold a liter of liquid. The jars are not completely filled with water, as shown. If the water from the two containers is combined, how many liters of water will there be altogether?
    (A) $1\frac{1}{4}$
    (B) $1\frac{7}{20}$
    (C) $1\frac{1}{2}$
    (D) $1\frac{3}{4}$

3. Travis had a board of wood that was $5\frac{2}{3}$ feet long. He cut off $2\frac{3}{5}$ feet of the board to make a birdhouse. How many feet long is the board now?
    (A) $2\frac{3}{5}$
    (B) $2\frac{4}{5}$
    (C) $3\frac{1}{20}$
    (D) $3\frac{1}{15}$

4. Use the pictures below to answer the question.

Circles are what fraction of the pictures?
(A) $\frac{1}{9}$
(B) $\frac{2}{9}$
(C) $\frac{1}{3}$
(D) $\frac{4}{9}$

5. The table below shows the items that Polly bought at the corner store for her trip to the beach.

Item	Price for One	Total Paid for Item
T-shirt	$5.25	$5.25
Bucket	$3.25	$6.50
Shovel	$1.50	$3.00
Bottle of water	$1.25	?

If Polly spent a total of $18.50, then how much did she spend on just bottles of water?
(A) $1.25
(B) $2.50
(C) $3.50
(D) $3.75

$14.75
+$ 3.75
18.50

6. The chart below shows the population of various towns.

Town	Population
Craigsville	9,782
Harriston	7,692
Montville	12,584
Kendrickson	4,312
Lionsville	2,409

Which town has a population that is about 1/3 that of Montville?
(A) Cragisville
(B) Harriston
(C) Kendrickson
(D) Lionsville

7. Use the number line below to answer the question.

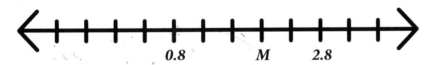

What value does point M represent?
(A) 1.1
(B) 2.0
(C) 2.2
(D) 2.4

8. Which fraction has the same value as 0.55?
(A) $\frac{55}{100}$
(B) $\frac{55}{10}$
(C) $\frac{55}{1000}$
(D) $\frac{1}{55}$

9. Which fraction is between $\frac{1}{2}$ and $\frac{4}{5}$?

   (A) $\frac{1}{5}$

   (B) $\frac{1}{3}$

   (C) $\frac{2}{5}$

   (D) $\frac{4}{7}$

10. Valerie invited ten children to her birthday party. Only five of them can come. What percent of the children Valerie invited are able to come to her party?

   (A) 25%

   (B) 50%

   (C) 75%

   (D) 100%

Answers to fractions, decimals, and percents practice set

1. A
2. C
3. D
4. C
5. D
6. C
7. B
8. A
9. D
10. B

Algebra

On the Lower Level ISEE, there are questions that test the basic principles of algebra. These questions require you to set up equations, solve, use the equations to find another value, etc.

The types of algebra questions you will see include:

- Setting up an equation to fit a story
- Input/output tables
- Solving for a variable
- Using proportion and scale
- Patterns
- Overlapping segments

Setting up an equation to fit a story

On the Lower Level ISEE, you may be asked to translate a story into an equation. These problems are really just testing your ability to identify which operation fits various situations.

- These questions are mainly testing which operation we use in different situations

These are a lot like the problems that we had in the whole numbers section only they now have variables in them. Variables are simply letters that stand in for some unknown quantity. They may also put in a shape instead of a letter for a variable.

- Variables are simply letters or shapes that stand in for some unknown number

Since we covered the basics of operations in the whole numbers section, let's just jump to some sample problems.

Here are some algebra questions like those that you will see on the ISEE:

1. Each box contains 5 packages of cookies. There are a total of 175 packages of cookies. If b represents the number of boxes, which equation could be used to figure out how many boxes of cookies there are?
   (A) $b = 5 \div 175$
   (B) $b = 175 \div 5$
   (C) $b - 175 = 5$
   (D) $b + 5 = 175$

To answer this question, we first have to think about which operation to use. We have a total number of packages (175), which are divided into equal groups of 5. This tells us that we should use division. That means that we can rule out choices C and D. Since we are given a total (175), then we need to divide the total by the size of each group (5) in order to figure out how many groups we have. Answer choice B correctly represents this.

2. At a restaurant, Lori bought a hamburger and two orders of French fries that cost $3 each. Her total before tax was $7. Which equation would find the cost of the hamburger (h)?
   (A) $2 + h = 7$
   (B) $2 + 3h = 7$
   (C) $2(3) + 2h = 7$
   (D) $2(3) + h = 7$

To answer this question, first think about how you would figure out the total if you did know the price of the hamburger. You would first take the cost of the French fries ($3) and multiply it by the number of orders of fries (2). Then you would add in the cost of the hamburger to get the total cost. Answer choice D correctly represents this, so it is the correct answer.

Sometimes questions will give you an equation and then ask you which story would fit the equation. For these questions, ruling out is the best approach.

- If the question asks you which story fits an equation, use ruling out

Here are a couple of examples of this type of question:

3. Which story would best fit the equation $2 \times 10 = 20$?
   (A) I have ten chocolates. I want to split the chocolates evenly between my two sisters. How many chocolates will each sister get?
   (B) I have two packages of chocolates. I ate ten chocolates from each package. How many chocolates did I eat?
   (C) I had ten chocolates. I gave away two of those chocolates. How many do I have left?
   (D) I had ten chocolates. My friend gave me two more. How many chocolates do I now have?

Let's start out by thinking about what multiplication means. We use multiplying when we know how many groups we have and how many are in each group. Multiplying gives us the total number. In the situation in choice A, the chocolates are being split into groups, so division would be more appropriate. We can rule out choice A. In choice B, we are given the number of packages, how many she ate from each group, and are asked to find the total. This fits multiplication very well, but let's just make sure there isn't a better answer choice. In choice C, we are given a total and then that total is reduced, so subtraction would be more appropriate. Choice C can be eliminated. For choice D, we are given a total and then that total is added to, so addition would be a better fit. Choice D is out. Answer choice B is the correct answer.

4. Myra writes down the following equation:

   $60 \div 12 = 5$

   Which question would best fit her equation?
   (A) There are 12 students in a class. Five of them did not do their homework. How many students did do their homework?
   (B) There are five classes and each class has twelve students. How many total students are there?
   (C) There were twelve students in each class, but five of them moved to another school. How many students are in each class now?
   (D) There are a total of sixty students in a school. They need to form teams for field day and each team must have twelve students. How many teams can be formed?

This is a division problem, so we are looking for a situation where items are being split into groups. In answer choice A, there are two groups, but they are not the same size. Division is appropriate when all the groups are the same size. Choice A can be eliminated. In answer choice B, the question asks for a total, which would fit with multiplication. Answer choice B can be ruled out. In answer choice C the total number is reduced, which would indicate subtraction, so choice C is out. In choice D we have the total number and then the group is divided into teams. This fits division perfectly, so answer choice D is the correct answer.

Some questions will not give you a story, but rather ask you to translate equation language into an actual equation. To answer these questions, follow the sentence word for word and translate into an equation. The only operation that can be a little tricky is subtraction. We often have to switch the order from the words to the equation for subtraction. For example, if we say "6 less than a number", we translate that as "$x - 6$" and NOT "$6 - x$".

- Translate questions word for word into numbers and symbols
- Be careful with subtraction- you may have to switch the order from the words to the equation

Here is a guide to some of the language you may see:

If the test says:	You should:
…more than…	use addition
…less than…	use subtraction
…divided by….	use division
…of…	use multiplication
…equal to…. OR …is…	insert an equal sign
…a number…	insert a variable

For example, let's say we have to turn the words "3 more than 5 times a number is equal to 7 less than that number". We would translate that as $3 + 5n = n - 7$.

Here are a couple of questions for you to try:

5. Larry needs to write an equation. His teacher tells him "4 times a number is 2 more than 3 times that same number". Which equation correctly represents this statement if Larry uses a B for the unknown number?
   (A) $(4 \times B) + 2 = 3x$
   (B) $(4 + B) + 2 = 3x$
   (C) $(4 \times B) = 2 + (3 \times B)$
   (D) $(4 \times B) = 2 \times (3 \times B)$

To answer this question, we need to just go word for word in translating. "4 times a number" would translate into "$(4 \times B)$", so we know that answer choice B can be eliminated. Then we have the word "is" so we know an equal sign comes next and answer choice A can also be ruled out. The next words are "2 more than". This would translate into "2+". We can eliminate choice D because it has multiplication at that point and not addition. We are left with answer choice C, which is correct.

6. Which equation would be read aloud as "4 more than 8 times a number is equal to 9 less than the number"? Use M to represent the number.
   (A) $4 + (8 \times M) = 9 - M$
   (B) $4 + (8 \times M) = M - 9$
   (C) $4 \times (8 \times M) = 9 - M$
   (D) $4 \times (8 \times M) = M - 9$

If we start at the beginning of the statement, the words "4 more" tell us that the correct answer choice will start with "4+". We can eliminate choices C and D. Now let's look at the differences between choices A and B. Answer choice A has $9 - M$ on the right hand side and answer choice B has $M - 9$ to the right of the equal sign. We have to remember to be careful since we see the words "less than". In this case, we have to put the variable first and then subtract the number. Answer choice B is correct.

Sometimes you will need to set up the equation and then solve. The trick to these questions is to remember to write down what your variable stands for. It is generally easiest if you define your variable as the thing that the question asks for.

- Remember to write down what your variable stands for
- Define your variable as the thing that the question asks for

For example, let's say that the question says, "In a pet store there are a total of 12 cats, dogs, and mice. If there are twice as many cats as dogs and three times as many mice as dogs, how many dogs are there in the pet store?". One way to solve would be to define our variable as being equal to the number of dogs since the question asks for the number of dogs.

Let $d = number\ of\ dogs$
$2d = number\ of\ cats$
$3d = number\ of\ mice$

Now that we have defined our variable, we can use the fact that there are a total of 12 animals.

$d + 2d + 3d = 12$
$6d = 12$
$d = 2$

By solving for our variable, we can see that there are 2 dogs in the pet store.

Here are a couple of questions for you to try:

7. Claire is making a mixture of cereal, pretzels, and chocolate candies. The combined weight of her mixture is 16 g. If the cereal weighs three times more than the pretzels and the chocolate candies weigh four times more than the pretzels, then how many grams do the pretzels weigh?
    (A) 1 g
    (B) 2 g
    (C) 6 g
    (D) 8 g

We can start out with defining our variable. Since the question asks how much the pretzels weigh, we will set our variable equal to the weight of the pretzels.

Let $p = the\ weight\ of\ the\ pretzels$
$3p = weight\ of\ the\ cereal$
$4p = weight\ of\ the\ chocolate\ candies$

Now we can use the fact that all together the mixture weighs 16g.

$p + 3p + 4p = 16$
$8p = 16$
$p = 2$

The pretzels weigh 2 g, so answer choice B is correct.

8. There are 27 students in a class. There are twice as many boys as there are girls. How many girls are in the class?
   (A) 6
   (B) 7
   (C) 9
   (D) 18

We can start out by defining our variable. The question asks for the number of girls, so we will set our variable equal to the number of girls.

$$\text{Let } g = number\ of\ girls$$
$$2g = number\ of\ boys$$
$$g + 2g = 27$$
$$3g = 27$$
$$g = 9$$

There are nine girls in the class, so answer choice C is correct.

Input/output tables

Another question type that you will see on the Lower Level ISEE asks you to use "input/output" machines. These questions are testing your ability to determine the rule used to get from one number to another. It may be a one-step machine- where you add/subtract/multiply/divide just once to get from one number to another. Keep in mind that there may be more than one step in the process, though. For example, the rule might be to multiply by 3 and then add 4. The trick is that the rule must work for all the input/output pairs.

- The rule may have one step, but it could also have two steps
- The rule must work for ALL input/output pairs

Here is an example of a basic input/output question:

1. Use the table below to answer the question.

Input Δ	Output $\boxtimes$
2	6
3	7
4	8
5	9

What is the rule that this function follows?
(A) $\Delta \times 3 = \boxtimes$
(B) $(\Delta \times 4) - 2 = \boxtimes$
(C) $(\Delta \times 2) + 2 = \boxtimes$
(D) $\Delta + 4 = \boxtimes$

The easiest way to approach this question is to plug in the inputs and outputs to the rules and see which one works. The trick is that if we plug in the first set of inputs and outputs, all the rules work. However, if we plug in the second set of inputs/outputs, then the only rule that works is answer choice D.

The next two questions are a little harder. You have to determine the rule on your own and then apply the rule to figure out the answer.

2. A number machine takes in an input number, performs the same operation on each number, and then prints an output number. The results are shown below.

Input	Output
21	7
18	6
15	5
9	3

Which input number would cause the machine to print 9?

(A) 3
(B) 9
(C) 27
(D) 36

Our first step is to figure out the operation that the machine is performing. If we look at just our first output, we might say that the machine subtracts 14 because $21 - 14 = 7$. However, if we look at our second output, we can see that rule does not work for all of the outputs. If we go back to the first output we could also say that the rule is to divide by 3. This works for all the inputs and outputs so we know that our rule is to divide by 3. Now we have to work backwards since the question gives us the output and asks for the input. To get from the output to the input, we would have to do the opposite operation, or multiply by 3 instead of dividing by 3. If we multiply 9 by 3, we get 27 as our answer. Choice C is the correct answer choice.

3. A number machine takes in an input number, performs the same operation on each number, and then prints an output number. The results are shown below.

Input	Output
20	9
18	8
16	7
14	6

If the number 10 was entered into the machine, what number would the machine print?

(A) 4
(B) 5
(C) 6
(D) 7

First we need to determine the rule. This question is a little harder because the input/output machine has a two-step rule. You have to play around with the numbers to see what works. For example, maybe you notice that to get from 20 to 9, you have to subtract 11. However, if you subtract 11 from 18, you do not get 8, so that cannot be the rule. Maybe you notice that all of the inputs are even, so you try to divide by 2. If you divide 20 by 2, you get 10. You would then have to subtract 1 to get the output of 9. Then you can try that same rule on the next input and output. If you divide 18 by 2, you get 9. You would then have to subtract 1 to get the output of 8. If you keep trying the rule of divide by 2, subtract 1, you will see that it works for all of the inputs and outputs. We now have to apply this rule to the number 10. If we divide 10 by 2 and then subtract 1, we get 4 as an answer. Answer choice A is the correct answer.

Solving for a variable

The basic goal of solving for a variable is to get a variable by itself –or to isolate it.

There are two basic rules for isolating a variable:

1. Use PEMDAS (order of operations), but in reverse
2. Do the opposite operation in each step

What does this mean to reverse the order of PEMDAS?

Here is a basic example:

$x + 2 = 4$ Using our reverse order of operations, first we look for addition or subtraction.

(In each step, notice that we do the *opposite* operation in order to simplify the equation.)

$x + 2 = 4$ The left side has *addition*, so we must *subtract*.
$\underline{-2 \ -2}$
$x = 2$ The problem is solved, the value of x is 2.

Here is another example:

$3 \times w = 9$ The left side is *multiplied* by 3 so we must *divide* by 3.
$\div 3 \ \div 3$
$w = 3$ The problem is solved. The value of w is 3.

On the ISEE, you may also see equations that are more than one step to solve. Just remember to follow the order of operations in reverse.

Here is an example:

$3 \times (b + 4) = 15$ Because we are doing PEMDAS in reverse order, we are going to save
$\div 3 \ \div 3$ the parentheses for LAST. We are going to do the opposite of multiplying by 3, which is dividing by 3.

$(b + 4) = 5$ Now we have to do the opposite of adding 4, which is to subtract 4
$\underline{-4 \ -4}$ from both sides.

$b = 1$ We can see that b is equal to 1.

Here is an example of how this type of question could look on the ISEE:

1.   If $16 = 4v + 4$, the v is equal to
     (A) 1
     (B) 2
     (C) 3
     (D) 4

In this question, we want to get v by itself. First we look for anything that is added or subtracted on the side of the equation that has v. There is a 4 added to the right side of the equation, so we have to subtract 4 from both sides. We are left with $12 = 4v$. Now we look for anything that is multiplied or divided. Currently, the v is multiplied by 4, so we have to divide both sides by 4. We are left with $v = 3$. Answer choice C is correct.

2. If $(8 \times \boxdot) + 2 = 5$, then what number could replace the $\boxdot$?
(A) $\frac{3}{8}$
(B) $\frac{6}{8}$
(C) 2
(D) 8

To solve, first we have to see if there is anything added or subtracted. There is a 2 added to the side with the variable, so we subtract that from both sides and get $8 \times \boxdot = 3$. Now we have an 8 that is multiplied by the variable, so we divide both sides by 8 and get $\boxdot = \frac{3}{8}$, so answer choice A is correct.

Some questions also require you to solve for more than one variable. Just remember to circle what the question is asking for since this is a multi-step problem.

Here is one for you to try:

3. Use the equations below to answer the question.
$8 + m = 10$
$6 + n = 10$

What is the value of $m + n$?
(A) 2
(B) 4
(C) 5
(D) 6

To answer this question we first have to solve for m and n. If $8 + m = 10$, then we know that m must be equal to 2 in order for the equation to be true. If $6 + n = 10$, then we can see that n must be equal to 4. Now we need to remember to add the values of m and n together in order to get our final answer. Since $2 + 4 = 6$, the correct answer is choice D.

Using proportion and scale

Another type of algebra question requires you to use proportions, which are basically just equivalent fractions. If a question gives you a rate, uses the word "per" or gives you the scale on a map or model, then you should use proportions.

- Use proportions for rate questions, if you see the word "per", or if the question gives you a scale

For example, a question may tell you that Sam can ride her bike 4 miles in 20 minutes and then asks how long it takes her to ride 6 miles at the same speed.

We can set up a proportion:

$$\frac{4\ miles}{20\ minutes} = \frac{6\ miles}{m\ minutes}$$

Now we can use cross-multiplying to solve for m.

$$4 \times m = 20 \times 6$$
$$4m = 120$$
$$\div 4 \quad \div 4$$
$$m = 30$$

We can see that it would take 30 minutes to ride 6 miles at the same speed. The trick to this type of question is to always write in units when you set up the equivalent fractions. In this question, that allowed us to easily see that if we put 4 miles on the top on the left side, we need to put 6 miles on the top on the right side.

- Always include units when you set up proportions so that you can make sure you put your variable in the right place

Here are a couple of questions for you to try:

1. Kim has a scale model airplane. The scale is that 0.8 inches on the model is equal to 10 feet on the actual airplane. If her model airplane is 2 inches long, then how long is the actual airplane?
   (A) 10 feet
   (B) 20 feet
   (C) 25 feet
   (D) 32 feet

In order to answer this question, we need to set up a proportion:

$$\frac{0.8 \; inches \; model}{10 \; feet \; actual} = \frac{2 \; inches \; model}{f \; feet \; actual}$$

Now we use cross-multiplying:

$$0.8 \times f = 10 \times 2$$
$$0.8f = 20$$
$$\div 0.8 \quad \div 0.8$$
$$f = 25$$

We can see that the actual airplane would be 25 feet long, so answer choice C is correct.

2. Juan and Clark are running at the same speed. It took Juan 12 minutes to run 1.5 miles. How long did it take Clark to run 2 miles?
(A) 16 minutes
(B) 20 minutes
(C) 24 minutes
(D) 32 minutes

Since this is a rate question, we set up a proportion in order to solve.

$$\frac{1.5 \; miles}{12 \; minutes} = \frac{2 \; miles}{m \; minutes}$$

Now we have to cross-multiply.
$$1.5 \times m = 2 \times 12$$
$$1.5m = 24$$
$$m = 16$$

We can see that it would take Clark 16 minutes to run 2 miles, so answer choice A is correct.

Patterns

On the ISEE, you may be asked to identify patterns. These questions aren't all that different from the input/output table questions. For these questions, you have to find the rule, just like you do for input/output questions.

- The trick to these questions is to find a rule, just like you did for the input/output questions

There are no hard and fast rules about how to determine what a pattern is on the ISEE. Is the same number added each time? Is one term multiplied by the same number each time to get the next term? Is it a multi-step pattern?

Here are some examples of how this could be tested on the ISEE:

1. Use the set of numbers below to answer the question.

    $$\left\{ \frac{1}{5}, \frac{2}{6}, \frac{3}{7}, \frac{4}{8}, ... \right\}$$

    What would be the next fraction in this pattern?
    (A) $\frac{1}{8}$
    (B) $\frac{2}{8}$
    (C) $\frac{3}{4}$
    (D) $\frac{4}{8}$

Look at the numerators (top numbers). Their pattern is to increase by 1 each time. The next numerator would be 4. Now look at the denominators (bottom numbers). They also get bigger by 1 each time, so the next denominator would be 8. Thus, the answer would be $4/8$, or answer choice D.

2. A number is 3 more than twice the previous number. The first number in the pattern is one. What is the 3rd number in the pattern?
    (A) 3
    (B) 5
    (C) 7
    (D) 13

    $(1 \times 2) + 3 = 5$

You start with the number 1. The directions say to take twice the number 1 and then add 3 to it. Twice the number 1 is 2, and then when you add 3 to it, you get 5. So 5 is the second number in the pattern. Now repeat the directions to find the next number, but start with the number 5. Take twice 5 and add 3. This gives 10 + 3, which is 13, so answer choice D is correct.

3. A number is said to be a square number if that number of objects can be arranged in rows such that a square can be built from the number of objects. Here is a diagram for the first three square numbers:

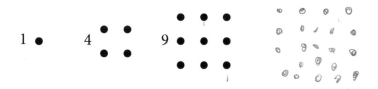

What are the next 2 square numbers?
(A) 10 and 12
(B) 16 and 20
(C) 16 and 25
(D) 25 and 36

To find this pattern, it is helpful to list out the parts of the pattern that we already have and look for the rule:

$$1st \, perfect \, square = 1 = 1 \times 1$$
$$2nd \, perfect \, square = 4 = 2 \times 2$$
$$3rd \, perfect \, square = 9 = 3 \times 3$$

Now it is easy to see how we would find the 4th perfect square- we would just multiply 4×4 and get 16. To find the fifth perfect square, we would just follow this pattern and multiply 5×5 to get 25. Answer choice C is correct.

4. Use the set below to answer the question.

    (4, 5, 7, 10, 14, 19, ...)

    What number would come next in this sequence?
    (A) 20
    (B) 25
    (C) 31
    (D) 39

First we to determine the pattern to the sequence. The difference between 4 and 5 is 1. To get from 5 to 7, we had to add 2. Then to get from 7 to 10, we had to add 3. We can see that the pattern is to add one more between each term. To get from 14 to 19, we had to add 5, so we will have to add 6 to get to the next term. Since 19 + 6 = 25, answer choice B is the correct answer.

Overlapping segments

The final type of algebra question that we will cover involves overlapping segments. These questions give you a picture and then ask you to see the algebraic relationship between the different pieces. The key to this type of question is to mark any information given in the question on the drawing.

- Mark any information given in the question onto the drawing

Here are some examples of this type of question:

1. Use the diagram below to answer the question.

    The distance between A and B is k units and the distance between B and C is j units. What is the distance between A and C?
    (A) j + k
    (B) j − k
    (C) k − j
    (D) j × k

Our first step is to add information from the question to the drawing. Our drawing should now look like this:

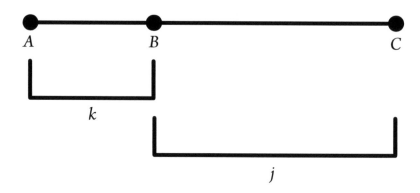

From this picture, we can now see that the length of *AC* would be equal to *j* and *k* added together. Answer choice A is the correct answer.

2. The length of *HJ* is *q* and the length of *HK* is *r*.

What is the length of JK?
(A) $q + r$
(B) $r - q$
(C) $q - r$
(D) $q \times r$

Our first step is to show on the drawing what the question gives us in words. Our drawing should now look like this:

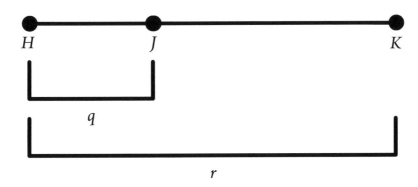

From this picture, it is easy to see that the length of JK would be the difference between r and q. That allows us to rule out answer choice A and D. Since a distance must be positive, we know that we must subtract the shorter distance (q) from the longer distance (r). Answer choice B is correct.

Those are the basics that you need to know about algebra questions on the Lower Level ISEE!

Be sure to complete the algebra practice set.

Algebra practice set

1. Use the equations below to answer the question.

$h + 2 = 6$
$k + 4 = 9$

What is the value of $k - h$?
(A) 1
(B) 2
(B) 3
(C) 9

2. Marty is creating a display in a grocery store. He is stacking boxes as shown below.

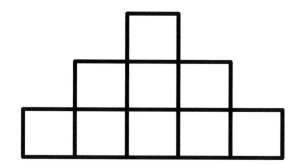

The first row has 1 box, the second row has 3 boxes, the third row has 5 boxes, and so on. How many boxes does the seventh row have?
(A) 7
(B) 8
(C) 11
(D) 13

3. A number machine reads input numbers and then performs the same operation on each number to create output numbers.

Input	Output
18	7
15	6
12	5
9	?

What output number would be created if the machine read the number 9 as an input number?

(A) 3
(B) 4
(C) 7
(D) 8

4. A box has 36 cans of sodas in it that are packaged in groups of 6. If p represents the number of packages of six cans, which equation could be used to figure out the number of packages in the box?

(A) $6 + p = 36$
(B) $p - 6 = 36$
(C) $p = 36 \div 6$
(D) $p = 36 \times 6$

5. What is the value of b in the equation $7 + 2b = 21$?

(A) 6
(B) 7
(C) 11
(D) 14

6. Use the diagram below to answer the question.

If the length of *DE* is 4 and the length of *DF* is 6, what is the length of *EF*?
(A) 2
(B) 3
(C) 4
(D) 6

7. Trisha can ride her bike 14 miles in 10 minutes. How many minutes would it take her to ride her bike for 21 miles?
(A) 13
(B) 15
(C) 18
(D) 20

8. What story would best fit the equation 24 ÷ 6 = 4?
(A) Sheila had 24 hats. She gave away 6 of them. How many does she have left?
(B) Sheila has 24 hats. She wants to split them into groups of 4. How many groups can she make?
(C) Sheila has 24 hats and her friend has 6 hats. How many hats do they have altogether?
(D) Sheila has 24 hats. She wants to split them into groups of 6. How many groups can she form?

9. The scale on a map shows that 8 miles is represented by 1.6 inches. How many miles would 2.4 inches represent?
(A) 8
(B) 10
(C) 12
(D) 14

10. Use the table below to figure out the rule for the function.

Input ■	Output Δ
3	8
4	11
5	14
6	17

What is the rule for this function?

(A) (■ × 3) − 1

(B) (■ × 3)+ 1

(C) (■ × 2) + 1

(D) (■ × 2) − 1

Answers to algebra practice set

1. A
2. D
3. B
4. C
5. B
6. A
7. B
8. D
9. C
10. A

Probability and Data Analysis

On the Lower Level ISEE, you will be expected to understand the basics of probability and to interpret data.

The types of questions that we will cover in this section include:

- Finding the probability of an event
- Using probability to work backwards
- Data- the two types
- Describing data- mean, median, mode, and range
- Different types of graphs and tables
- Venn Diagrams
- Using data to make predictions

Finding the probability of an event

You may see questions that ask you the probability of an event happening. It might be the probability of drawing a certain card or of a certain person being chosen. You might also see the word "chance", such as "what is the chance of drawing a card with a 3 on it?"

- If you see the word "chance" it is also a probability question

The basic formula for finding probability (or chance) is:

$$\frac{number\ of\ outcomes\ that\ you\ want}{total\ number\ of\ outcomes}$$

For example, let's say we have a box of candies. There are 8 red candies, 4 green candies, and 2 yellow candies.

The probability of picking a yellow candy would be:

$$\frac{number\ of\ outcomes\ that\ you\ want}{total\ number\ of\ outcomes} = \frac{2}{14}$$

A probability can also be reduced, so we would reduce $\frac{2}{14}$ in order to get our final answer.

$$\frac{2 \div 2}{14 \div 2} = \frac{1}{7}$$

We could also say that the chance of picking a yellow candy is 1 out of 7.

The most basic type of probability question asks you to determine probability from a picture. These questions are just like the fraction problems that we did earlier with pictures.

Here is an example:

1. Use the pictures below to answer the question.

If a shape is chosen at random, what is the chance that it will be a ♡?
(A) 1 out of 3
(B) 1 out of 4
(C) 2 out of 7
(D) 3 out of 10

In order to answer this question, we first have to count up the total number of shapes. There are a total of 12 shapes, so we know that will be the bottom number in our fraction (even though the answer choices are not given in fraction form, it is easier to start there in order to reduce). Now we have to count up how many there are of the shape that we want to choose. There are 3 heart shapes, so that becomes the top number in our fraction.

$$\frac{number\ of\ outcomes\ that\ you\ want}{total\ number\ of\ outcomes} = \frac{3}{12}$$

Now we have to reduce the probability.

$$\frac{3 \div 3}{12 \div 3} = \frac{1}{4}$$

We can see that the probability of choosing a heart shape is $\frac{1}{4}$ and another way to write that is 1 out of 4. Answer choice B is the correct answer.

Some other questions will require you to figure out a total first and then determine a probability.

Here are a couple of examples:

2. Trevor has a deck of cards that are labeled A through M. If none of the cards are repeated, what is the chance that the first card he picks will have the letter L on it?
    (A) $\frac{9}{26}$
    (B) $\frac{3}{11}$
    (C) $\frac{1}{13}$
    (D) $\frac{1}{26}$

Our first step is to figure out how many total cards we have. If we count up the letters A through M, we get that there must be 13 total cards. Since only one of these cards has the letter L on it, the probability of choosing the letter L would be $\frac{1}{13}$. Answer choice C is correct.

3. Kevin has a bowl with chocolate covered candies in it. There are red, yellow, green, blue, and brown candies. If there are 4 red candies, 5 yellow candies, 10 green candies, 7 blue candies, and 4 brown candies, which color has a $\frac{1}{6}$ probability of being chosen?
    (A) red
    (B) yellow
    (C) green
    (D) blue

In order to find a probability, we first have to find the total number of candies. If we add $4 + 5 + 10 + 7 + 4$, we get that there are 30 candies in the bowl. Now we have to figure out the probability of choosing each color. Let's start with answer choice A- red. There are 4 red candies, so the probability of choosing a red candy would be $\frac{4}{30}$. This is not in reduced form, however, so we need to reduce the probability to see if it is equal to $\frac{1}{6}$. If we reduce the fraction, we get $\frac{4 \div 2}{30 \div 2} = \frac{2}{15}$, which is not equal to $\frac{1}{6}$, so answer choice A can be eliminated. Now let's try answer choice B. There are 5 yellow candies, so the probability of choosing a yellow candy would be $\frac{5}{30}$.

Now we have to reduce this probability: $\frac{5 \div 5}{30 \div 5} = \frac{1}{6}$. Since this is the probability that we were looking for, answer choice B is correct.

Using probability to work backwards

Some questions will give you a probability and then expect you to work backwards to find the number of events.

To answer these questions, just set up proportions and then solve. Just like we did in the proportions section, be sure to label each number so that you can be sure you are putting the variable in the right place.

- Set up a proportion
- Remember to label each number

The easiest of this problem type gives you a probability for choosing an item and then asks you for either the total number of that item or the total number of items. Just remember to set up the proportion to solve.

Here are a couple of examples:

1. Gillian has yellow pencils and blue pencils in a box. The probability of choosing a yellow pencil is 2 out of 5. If there are 8 yellow pencils, how many total pencils are in the box?
   (A) 2
   (B) 8
   (C) 12
   (D) 20

Let's set up a proportion in order to solve. We will put the probability on the left side of the equal sign and the actual number of pencils on the right side of the equal sign.

$$\frac{2 \; yellow \; pencils}{5 \; total \; pencils} = \frac{8 \; yellow \; pencils}{p \; total \; pencils}$$

Now we use cross-multiplying in order to solve.

$$2 \times p = 8 \times 5$$
$$2p = 40$$

$$p = 20$$

There are 20 total pencils, so answer choice D is correct.

2. Forest has a bouquet with pink, yellow, and white flowers in it. If he randomly chooses a flower, then the probability that it will be white is 4 out of 9. If there are 36 total flowers, how many of them are white?
(A) 16
(B) 20
(C) 30
(D) 36

We will start with setting up a proportion.

$$\frac{4\ white}{9\ total} = \frac{w\ white\ flowers}{36\ total\ flowers}$$

Now we will cross-multiply.

$$4 \times 36 = 9 \times w$$
$$144 = 9w$$
$$16 = w$$

There are 16 white flowers in the bouquet, so answer choice A is correct.

Sometimes probability questions that require working backward are a little harder. The question might give you one probability and then ask you for how many there are of a different item. The important thing to keep in mind is that all of the probabilities must add to 1.

For example, let's say we have green and blue towels. If the probability of choosing a green towel is 2 out of 5 that means that if we randomly pick 5 towels, 2 of them will probably be green. The flip side of this statement is that 3 of them would be blue. If we convert these probabilities to fractions, we can see that they add to 1:

$$\frac{2}{5} + \frac{3}{5} = 1$$

The key to these questions is to remember that they are multi-step problems. We can't just find the first answer and stop there.

- These are multi-step problems, don't choose the answer from the first step!

Here are some examples for you to try:

3. Carlos has baseball hats and cowboy hats. If he randomly draws a hat, the probability that it will be a baseball hat is 2 out of 3. If he has a total of 18 hats in his collection, how many of them are cowboy hats?
    (A) 6
    (B) 9
    (C) 12
    (D) 18

One possible way to start this problem is to figure out the probability of choosing a cowboy hat. If the probability of choosing a baseball hat is $\frac{2}{3}$ and we know that the probabilities have to add to 1, then we can see that the probability of choosing a cowboy hat is $\frac{1}{3}$. Now we can use that probability to find the number of cowboy hats.

$$\frac{1 \; cowboy \; hat}{3 \; total \; hats} = \frac{c \; cowboy \; hats}{18 \; total \; hats}$$

$$1 \times 18 = 3 \times c$$
$$18 = 3c$$
$$6 = c$$

Answer choice A is correct.

4. Vickie bought a bunch of red and blue balloons for a party. If she were to randomly choose a balloon, the probability of choosing a red balloon would be 4 out of 7. There are 15 blue balloons in the bunch. How many red balloons are there?
    (A) 15
    (B) 20
    (C) 30
    (D) 35

This one is definitely a multi-step problem. Let's start with the information that we are given. We are given the probability of choosing a red balloon, but we are also given the total number of blue balloons. In order to solve, we need to first figure out the probability of choosing a blue balloon. If 4 out of 7 balloons are red, then 3 out of 7 would be blue. Now we can use this probability to solve for how many total balloons there are. We set up a proportion with the probability on the left and the actual numbers of balloons on the right:

$$\frac{3 \; blue \; balloons}{7 \; total \; balloons} = \frac{15 \; blue \; balloons}{b \; total \; balloons}$$

Now we use cross-multiplying to solve for the total number of balloons.

$$3 \times b = 7 \times 15$$
$$3b = 105$$
$$b = 35$$

We know that there are 35 total balloons. Of those balloons, 15 are blue. To find the number of red balloons, we have to subtract the number of blue balloons from the total.

$$35 - 15 = 20$$

There are 20 red balloons, so answer choice B is correct.

Finally, we have a problem type that is tough. This problem type gives us a probability and then asks us to break down that probability into parts. The trick to these questions is to remember that the total includes the item that we are looking for.

For example, let's say that we have two items to choose between:

$$probability \; of \; choosing \; 1st \; item = \frac{\# \; of \; 1st \; items}{total \; \# \; of \; all \; items} =$$

$$\frac{\# \; of \; 1st \; items}{\# \; of \; 1st \; items + \# \; of \; 2nd \; items}$$

We just have to remember that a probability is given as a part out of the whole, but the answer choices may gives us the parts and we have to find the whole on our own.

Here are a couple of examples:

5. A bag has red bouncy balls and blue bouncy balls in it. If a ball is chosen at random, the probability that the ball will be blue is 5 out of 9. Which combination could be the number of red and blue balls in the bag?
    (A) 4 red balls and 5 blue balls
    (B) 5 red balls and 4 blue balls
    (C) 4 red balls and 9 blue balls
    (D) 5 red balls and 9 blue balls

We have to remember that a probability gives us part out of the whole. This means that if 5 out of the 9 balls are blue, then 4 out of the 9 balls would be red. Answer choice A gives us 4 red balls and 5 blue balls, so that works with the probability that we were given. Answer choice A is correct.

6. Mike has a box of cupcakes with different flavors of frosting: vanilla, buttercream, lemon, and chocolate. The probability of choosing a cupcake with buttercream frosting is 2 out of 7. What could be the combination of cupcakes in the box?
    (A) 2 buttercream and 7 others
    (B) 6 buttercream and 21 others
    (C) 6 buttercream and 15 others
    (D) 15 buttercream and 45 others

To answer this question we have to convert the answer choices into a fraction that compares the part to the whole instead of part to part. Let's start with choice A:

$$\frac{buttercream}{total} = \frac{2}{2+7} = \frac{2}{9}$$

We can see that the probability of choosing a buttercream cupcake with choice A would be 2 out of 9. Since this is not 2 out of 7, we can rule out choice A.

Now let's try choice B:

$$\frac{buttercream}{total} = \frac{6}{6+21} = \frac{6}{27}$$

Now we have to reduce this probability in order to see if it matches the 2 out of 7 that we are looking for.

$$\frac{6 \div 3}{27 \div 3} = \frac{2}{9}$$

Again, we got a probability of 2 out of 9, so we can eliminate choice B.

Now let's try choice C:

$$\frac{buttercream}{total} = \frac{6}{6 + 15} = \frac{6}{21}$$

Let's reduce this probability and see if it is 2 to 7.

$$\frac{6 \div 3}{21 \div 3} = \frac{2}{7}$$

The probability is 2 out of 7! Answer choice C is correct.

Data- the two types

There are two different types of data- numerical and categorical.

Numerical data can also be called quantitative data. It consists of data that can be measured using numbers. For example, inches of plant growth would be numerical data because inches can be measured with a ruler.

- Numerical (or quantitative) data can be measured

The second type of data is categorical, or qualitative, data. This kind of data is sorted by some sort of category or characteristic. For example, sorting plants by type of plant would be categorical.

On the Lower Level ISEE, they probably will ask you to apply this information. You may not have any questions at all that test this difference, however.

Here are a couple of examples of questions that test the difference between the two types of data:

1. Kendra has an assignment to poll her class and then make a graph from the results. Which would be the best question to ask if she wants to make a bar graph?
   (A) Who is your favorite singer?
   (B) How many minutes a night do you read?
   (C) Where do you go shopping?
   (D) What states have you been to?

In order to make a bar graph, it is best to ask a numerical question. We are looking for a question that students could respond to with a number. Only answer choice B asks for a number, so it is the correct answer choice.

2. Lorraine's class is going to a local pond to collect data about the habitat. The students needed to list what they saw in categories.

> **LORRAINE'S OBSERVATIONS**
> 1. Types of plants: grasses, water plants, trees, bushes
> 2. Animals seen in the water: frogs, fish, insects
> 3. ?

Which information would best complete Lorraine's observation list?
(A) number of lily pads
(B) dimensions of the pond
(C) birds observed at the pond
(D) heights of various plants

If we look at the observation list, we can see that all of the data is categorical. It is not listing out specific numbers, but rather dividing the observations into groups. We are looking for another observation that is a category. Answer choice C is the only answer choice that does not ask for specific numbers, so it is the correct answer choice.

Describing data- mean, median, mode, and range

There are several different ways to describe data.

Here is a cheat sheet for the terms that you will need to know for the Lower Level ISEE:

- **Mean:** the average. Add up all of the numbers and then divide by the number of numbers.
- **Median:** the middle number. Put the numbers in order from least to greatest. The middle number is the median. If there is an even number of numbers, the median is the average of the two middle numbers.
- **Mode:** the most common number. The mode is the number or numbers that show up most often. There can be more than one mode, or there can be no mode if no number shows up more than once.
- **Range:** the difference between the largest and the smallest numbers.

To find the mean of a set of data, we add up the numbers and divide by the number of numbers. For example, let's say we need to find the mean of 3, 4, 5, and 6. First, we find the sum:

$$3 + 4 + 5 + 6 = 18$$

Now we need to divide that by 4 since we have 4 numbers.

$$\frac{18}{4} = 4\frac{1}{2}$$

The mean of our numbers is $4\frac{1}{2}$.

Here is a question that tests mean:

1. Chloe has four bags of beans. Two of the bags weigh $2\frac{1}{4}$ pounds each, one bag weighs $1\frac{1}{2}$ pounds, and one bag weighs 3 pounds. What is the mean weight of the bags of beans?
    (A) $1\frac{1}{2}$ pounds
    (B) 2 pounds
    (C) $2\frac{1}{4}$ pounds
    (D) $2\frac{1}{2}$ pounds

Our first step in finding the mean weight is to add all of the weights together. It is important that we remember to add $2\frac{1}{4}$ twice because there are two bags of that weight.

$$2\frac{1}{4} + 2\frac{1}{4} + 1\frac{1}{2} + 3 = 9$$

Now we have to divide the sum by the number of numbers and then simplify:

$$\frac{9}{4} = \frac{4}{4} + \frac{4}{4} + \frac{1}{4} = 2\frac{1}{4}$$

Answer choice C is correct.

Some questions test a deeper understanding of mean or average. If there are only two numbers, then the average (or mean) is halfway in between the two numbers.

Here are some examples of questions that test this concept:

2. The average length of two books is 180 pages. If one book has 200 pages, how many pages does the other book have?
(A) 160
(B) 180
(C) 200
(D) 220

If the average length of the two books is 180 pages, then one book must have more than 180 pages and the other book must have less than 180 pages. Since we know that one book has 200 pages, which is more than 180, then we know that the unknown book must have less than 180 pages. Only answer choice A has less than 180 pages, so it is the correct answer choice. Another way to think about this is that 200 pages is 20 pages more than the average, so the other book must be 20 pages less than the average. 160 is 20 less than 180, so answer choice A is the right answer.

3. Use the number line below.

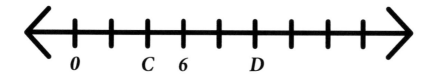

Point D is the average of C and another number. What is that other number?
(A) 0
(B) 8
(C) 10
(D) 16

Since this is a number line problem, our first step is to figure out what the number line is counting by. There are three segments between 0 and 6, so the number line must be counting by 2's. That means that C must be equal to 4 and D must be equal to 10. If D is the average of C and another number, D must be halfway in between C and the other number. If we count up from C, we can see that the difference between C and D is 6. If we keep counting another 6 numbers, then we get to the other number. The other number is 16. Answer choice D is correct.

You may also see a question that asks you to find a median. In order to find a median, you need to list the numbers in order from least to greatest. If there are an even number of numbers, then take the average of the two middle numbers.

Here are a couple of questions that test median:

4. Katie's class is recording the highest recorded temperature each day for one week.

Day	Highest Recorded Temperature (in degrees)
Sunday	58
Monday	62
Tuesday	54
Wednesday	69
Thursday	65
Friday	59
Saturday	61

What was the median temperature this week?
(A) 58
(B) 59
(C) 61
(D) 62

Our first step is to put the temperatures in order. It would look like this:

54, 58, 59, 61, 62, 65, 69

Now we have to find the middle number. There are 3 numbers that are less than 61 and three numbers that are greater than 61, so 61 is the median temperature for the week. Answer choice C is correct.

5.   During the month of August, the bike shop sold 6 bikes. Their prices are listed below.

Bike #1	$25
Bike #2	$29
Bike #3	$24
Bike #4	$28
Bike #5	$26
Bike #6	$30

What was the median price of the bikes that sold in August?
(A) $26
(B) $27
(C) $28
(D) $29

To find the median, first we have to put the prices in order. It would look like this:

24, 25, 26, 28, 29, 30

There are an even number of numbers, so our next step is to average the two middle numbers. The two middle numbers are 26 and 28.

$$\frac{26 + 28}{2} = \frac{54}{2} = 27$$

Answer choice B is correct.

Another way we can describe data is with the mode. The mode of a set of data is the number that shows up the most often. A data can have more than one mode, or it can have no mode at all if there are no numbers that repeat in the data set.

Here is an example of a question that tests mode:

6. Jerry made a table of his test scores for the last quarter.

JERRY'S TEST SCORES				
Math	93	89	87	81
English	90	93	85	93
Biology	89	81	93	85
History	81	93	85	87

What is the mode of this set of data?
(A) 81
(B) 85
(C) 89
(D) 93

We are looking for the number that shows up most often in the data. The easiest way to figure this out is to make our own chart.

Number	How many times it shows up
81	3
85	3
87	2
89	2
90	1
93	5

When we rearrange the data this way, we can see that the number 93 shows up the most often, so it is the mode.

Sometimes there will be a question that tests mode, but the question does not actually use the word "mode".

Here is an example:

7. Zara took a poll of the students in her class and asked them to vote for one of four different ice cream flavors. She is going to have a party and wants to serve the ice cream flavor that is most popular with her classmates.

Flavor	Number of Votes
Vanilla	5
Chocolate	10
Butter Pecan	2
Strawberry	8

What flavor ice cream should Zara serve at her party?
(A) Vanilla
(B) Chocolate
(C) Butter Pecan
(D) Strawberry

Since Zara wants to serve the most popular ice cream flavor, she should choose the flavor that got the most votes, or the mode of the data set. More students chose chocolate than any other flavor, so answer choice B is correct.

The last term that you will need to know for describing data is range. Range is the difference between the smallest number and the largest number in a set of data.

Range = largest # − smallest #

For example, let's say we have the numbers 8, 3, 9, 11, and 2. The largest number in the set is 11 and the smallest number is 2. To find the range, we would subtract 2 from 11, and get that the range of the data set is 9.

Here is a question that tests range:

8. Use the following set of numbers to answer the question:

    $\{2, 6, 9, 7, 5, 5\}$

    What is the range of this data?
    (A) 5
    (B) $5\frac{2}{3}$
    (C) 6
    (D) 7

In order to find the range, we first have to identify the largest number in the set and the smallest number in the set. The largest number is 9 and the smallest number is 2. The range is *largest # − smallest # = 9 − 2 = 7*. Answer choice D is correct.

Finally, here is a question that puts it all together:

9. James recorded the number of games won for each team in his baseball league. The graph below shows the results.

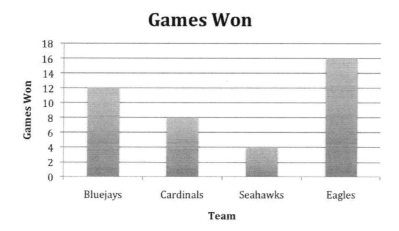

Based on this graph, which of the following conclusions is true?
(A) The Bluejays won fewer games than the Cardinals.
(B) The mode of this data is 10.
(C) The mean number of games won is between 9 and 10.
(D) The range is greater than the number of games that the Cardinals won.

The best way to answer this question is to use ruling out. If we look at choice A, it is obvious that the Bluejays won MORE games than the Cardinals, so we can eliminate choice A. There is no mode to this data since no number shows up more than once. We can eliminate choice B. To evaluate choice C, we first have to find the mean. This requires us to add up all the data: $12 + 8 + 4 + 16 = 40$. Now we divide that sum by the number of numbers: $\frac{40}{4} = 10$. We now know that the mean of the data is 10, which means it is NOT between 9 and 10. Answer choice C can be eliminated. Finally, we have choice D. The range of this data is *largest # − smallest #* $= 16 − 4 = 12$. Since 12 is greater than 8 (the number of games that the Cardinals won), answer choice D is correct.

Different types of graphs and tables

On the Lower Level ISEE, you will see several different ways to represent data.

The ones that you are most likely to see include:

- Bar graphs
- Line graphs
- Pie charts
- Pictographs

Line graphs and bar graphs are pretty straightforward. You just find what the question is asking about on the x-axis and follow it across to the y-axis to find the value. The only trick to line and bar graphs is to make sure you know the scale that is used on each axis. The lines on a graph don't always count by one, they could count by 2, 5 or some other number.

- Check the scale with line and bar graphs

Here is an example of how a bar graph question could look:

1. Jared recorded the number of minutes that he rode his bike for five days in the graph below.

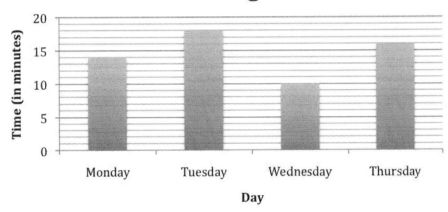

Number of Minutes Spent Bike Riding

Which statement is true?
(A) Jared rode for 4 more minutes on Monday than he did on Tuesday.
(B) Jared rode for longer on Tuesday than he did on Monday and Wednesday combined.
(C) Jared rode for 6 more minutes on Thursday than he did on Wednesday.
(D) Jared rode for the most minutes on Thursday.

Let's use ruling out to answer this question. Jared rode for 14 minutes on Monday and 18 minutes on Tuesday. He rode for 4 minutes less on Monday than he did on Tuesday, so we can eliminate choice A. On Wednesday, he rode for 10 minutes. If we combine the time he rode on Monday (14 minutes) and the time he rode on Wednesday (10 minutes), then we get 24 minutes. This is greater than the time that he rode on Tuesday (18 minutes), so answer choice B can be eliminated. Jared rode for 16 minutes on Thursday, which is 6 more minutes than he rode on Wednesday (10 minutes). Answer choice C is the correct answer.

Here is an example of a question that uses a line graph:

2. Mr. Galen's class measured the outside temperature throughout a school day. They recorded their findings in the graph below.

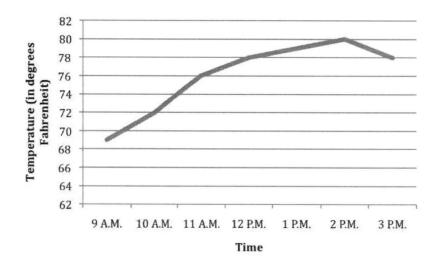

What was the range of temperatures that Mr. Galen's class recorded?
(A) 8 degrees
(B) 9 degrees
(C) 10 degrees
(D) 11 degrees

To find the range, we have to first figure out what the highest and lowest recorded temperatures were. The highest temperature was recorded at 2 P.M. and it was 80 degrees. The lowest temperature was recorded at 9 A.M. and it was 69 degrees. The range is equal to 80 − 69, or 11 degrees. Answer choice D is correct.

The next type of graph that you may see is a pie chart, which is also called a circle graph. A pie chart shows data in fractional pieces.

Here are some basic conversions between pie charts and fractions:

$\frac{1}{4} = 25\% =$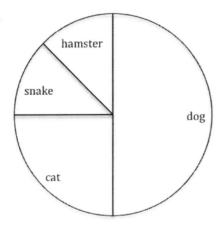

$\frac{1}{2} = 50\% =$

$\frac{3}{4} = 75\% =$

Some pie chart questions simply ask you to translate into fractional pieces. These questions are just like the questions that we did in the fraction section with pictures. We simply have to divide the circle into even pieces.

Here is an example:

3. Patrick asked his friends what kinds of pets they have in their homes. Their answers are displayed in the circle graph below.

About what fraction of his friends have a hamster in their home?
(A) $\frac{1}{8}$
(B) $\frac{1}{4}$
(C) $\frac{1}{3}$
(D) $\frac{1}{2}$

The easiest way to answer this question is to divide the chart into equal parts.

It would look like this:

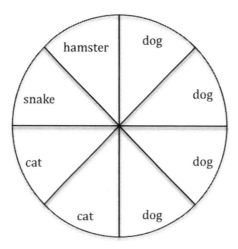

From this graph, we can see that there are 8 equal parts in this graph. Since hamsters take up just 1 out of these 8 pieces, $\frac{1}{8}$ of Jared's friends said that they had a hamster. Answer choice A is correct.

Questions that are a little harder are those that ask you to convert between a fraction on a circle graph and an actual number. To answer these questions, we need to multiply the fraction from the circle graph by the total number.

- If you are given a circle graph and they ask for the actual number for one of the sections, multiply the fraction that section takes up by the total number given

Here is an example of a question of this type:

4. There are 600 students at Smith Elementary School. The circle graph below shows how each student got to school this morning.

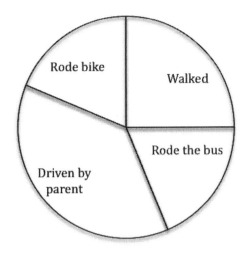

About how many students at Smith Elementary walked to school this morning?
(A) 150
(B) 200
(C) 300
(D) 400

To answer this question, we first have to figure out what fraction of the students walked to school this morning. If we look just at the section that represents students who walk, we can see that about $\frac{1}{4}$ of the students walked to school. There are 600 total students so we multiply $\frac{1}{4}$ by 600 and get that 150 students walked to school. Answer choice A is the correct answer.

The final type of question is even trickier. The question gives you the value of for one segment of the graph and asks you to find the value of another segment. For these questions, it is usually easier to compare the section you are given to the section the question asks for rather than trying to do a lot of complicated math.

- If they give you one segment and then ask for another, see if you can just compare and use ruling out to answer the question

Here is an example:

5. Use the graph below to answer the question.

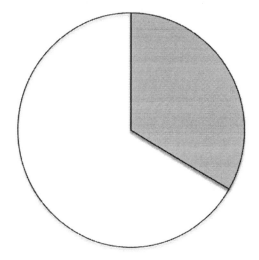

If the shaded portion of the graph represents 12,000 people, how many people are represented by the unshaded portion of the graph?
(A) 6,000
(B) 12,000
(C) 15,000
(D) 24,000

Let's start out by comparing the shaded portion to the unshaded portion. The unshaded portion is about twice as big as the shaded region. That means that it would represent about twice as many people, or 2 × 12,000. Since 2 × 12,000 = 24,000, answer choice D is correct.

Another type of graph that you may see on the Lower Level ISEE is a pictograph.

A pictograph uses a figure to represent a number of items. The important thing to remember with pictograph questions is that you have to use the key. The key tells you how many items each picture stands for. For example, a chart might give different types of books in the library. Maybe there are three books shown for the science section, but each book picture stands for 6,000 books. This tells us that there are really 18,000 science books in the library.

- Do not forget to use the key on pictograph questions!

Here is an example of how these questions look on the ISEE:

6. A coffee shop has four different locations. The chart below shows how many cups of coffee are sold each day in the different locations.

CUPS OF COFFEE SOLD	
Greentown	
Redburg	
Blueville	
Yellowton	

 = 750 cups of coffee

How many more cups of coffee are sold in Greentown than in Blueville?
(A) 1
(B) 750
(C) 1,500
(D) 2,250

The important thing to remember in answering this question is that one coffee cup in the pictograph does not represent one cup of coffee sold. The key at the bottom tells us that one picture of a coffee cup is really equal to 750 cups of coffee sold. There is one more cup of coffee in the Greentown row than in the Blueville row, so there were 750 more cups of coffee sold in Greentown than in Blueville and answer choice B is correct.

You may even get a question where the key is not given, but you need to come up with it yourself. Setting up a proportion is generally the best way to answer these questions. Just remember that when we set up proportions, we label the top and the bottom of the fraction so that we can keep it all straight.

- You may have to figure out what the scale is on your own
- The easiest way to answer these questions is to set up a proportion

Here is an example:

7. Use the pictograph below to answer the question.

NUMBER OF GRADUATES	
Hill University	🎓🎓🎓🎓🎓🎓
Eastern University	🎓🎓🎓🎓🎓🎓🎓
Coastal College	🎓🎓🎓
Mountain College	🎓🎓🎓🎓

If 900 students graduated from Mountain College, how many students graduated from Hill University?

(A) 6
(B) 675
(C) 1,100
(D) 1,350

In order to answer this question, we use the data that we are given and set up a proportion.

$$\frac{4 \; hats \; for \; Mountain \; College}{900 \; students \; at \; Mountain \; College} = \frac{6 \; hats \; for \; Hill \; University}{s \; students \; at \; Hill \; University}$$

Now, since it is a proportion, we can use cross-multiplying to solve.

$$4 \times s = 900 \times 6$$
$$4s = 5400$$
$$\div 4 \qquad \div 4$$
$$s = 1350$$

Answer choice D is the correct answer.

Venn Diagrams

On the ISEE, you often see questions that test Venn Diagrams. Venn Diagrams show overlapping circles.

Here is an example:

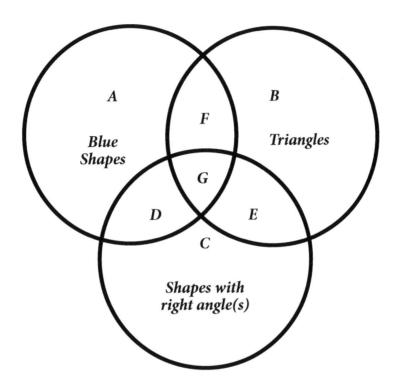

In the above diagram, a blue triangle that does not have a right angle would go in section F. It has the characteristics of the blue shapes circle and the triangles circle, so it would go where the two overlap. It does not have a right angle, however, so it would not go in section G. A yellow square would go in section C. It has right angles, but it is not blue and is not a triangle, so it would belong in the section of the "shapes with right angle(s)" circle that does not overlap the other sections.

Here are some examples of Venn Diagram questions like those you may see on the ISEE:

1. Use the Venn Diagram below to answer the question.

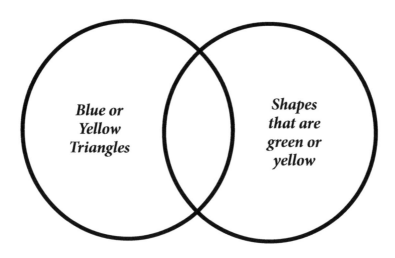

What shape would be found in the area where the two circles overlap?
(A) A yellow square
(B) A green triangle
(C) A yellow triangle
(D) A blue rectangle

Let's use ruling out to answer this question. If we look at choice A, a yellow square would definitely fit within the "shapes that are green and yellow circle", but we need a shape that would fit within both circles. We can rule out choice A because it would not fit within the "blue or yellow triangles" circle. If we look at choice B, a green triangle would not fit within the "blue or yellow triangles" circle, so we can eliminate it. If we look at choice C, a yellow triangle would fit within the categories of both "blue or yellow triangles" and "shapes that are green or yellow", so it is the correct answer choice.

2. Use the Venn Diagram below to answer the question.

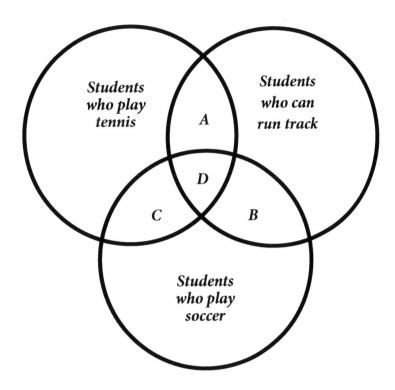

Carlos plays soccer and tennis, but does not run track. In what region should his name be written?

(A) Region A
(B) Region B
(C) Region C
(D) Region D

We are looking for the region where "students who play tennis" and "students who play soccer" overlap. This is true for both regions C and D. However, region D includes students who run track. Since Carlos does not run track, we can eliminate region D. The correct answer is region C, or choice C.

Using data to make predictions

You may or may not see a question on the ISEE that asks you to make a prediction from data. Basically, you want to just look for trends in the data given and then continue those trends.

Here is an example of a question that asks you to predict data:

1. A class planted three sunflowers. One sunflower was placed in a dark room, one sunflower was put under a grow lamp that was left on all the time, and one sunflower was placed outside in a sunny spot. Each day, the class measured the sunflowers. The data they collected is shown below.

	Dark location	Under grow lamp	In a sunny spot
Day 1	0 in.	1 in.	0 in.
Day 2	0 in.	3 in.	1 in.
Day 3	0 in.	7 in.	1 in.
Day 4	0 in.	9 in.	2 in.
Day 5	0 in.	12 in.	3 in.

If the plants continue to follow the same pattern of growth, what would be the predicted height of the sunflower under the grow lamp on Day 7?
(A) 12 in.
(B) 14 in.
(C) 17 in.
(D) 20 in.

If we look at the growth pattern, we can see that the plant under the grow lamp grows about 2-3 inches a day. Between Day 5 and Day 7, two days go by. We would expect the plant to grow between 4 and 6 inches in two days. Since the plant is at 12 inches on day 5, if we add 4 to 6 inches to that height, we get that the plant should be between 16 and 18 inches tall. Only answer choice C falls within this range, so that is the correct answer.

Now you know how to handle probability and data questions. Be sure to complete the practice set!

Probability and data practice set

1. Carla has a bag of marbles. In her bag there are 6 red marbles, 4 blue marbles, 8 green marbles, and 6 yellow marbles. If she picks a marble randomly, what are the odds that she will pick a blue marble?
    (A) 1 in 4
    (B) 1 in 6
    (C) 1 in 8
    (D) 3 in 12

2. Jerry's class had to collect data from objects around their classroom. The students had to list their observations in categories or groups.

    > **JERRY'S OBSERVATIONS**
    > 1. kinds of books in the library
    > 2. colors of backpacks
    > 3. ?

    What information would complete Jerry's list of observations?
    (A) number of desks
    (B) height of chairs
    (C) dimensions of classroom
    (D) types of writing instruments in the art drawer

3. Use the number line given below to answer the question.

    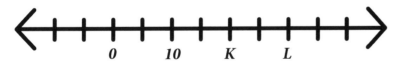

    L is the average of K and another number. What is that other number?
    (A) 16
    (B) 20
    (C) 40
    (D) 50

4. Mr. Thomas' class is making candy. They mixed sugar and water and put it into a pan with a candy thermometer attached to the inside. This pan was put on a hot burner. They recorded the temperature reading every minute.

Time	Temperature
1 min	90°
2 min	120°
3 min	149°
4 min	183 °

The class has to remove the pan from the heat when the sugar and water mixture reaches 290°. About how many minutes after they put the pan on the burner will the water and sugar mixture reach 290°?

(A) between 7 and 9 minutes

(B) between 10 and 12 minutes

(C) between 12 and 13 minutes

(D) between 14 and 16 minutes

5. Use the Venn Diagram below to answer the question.

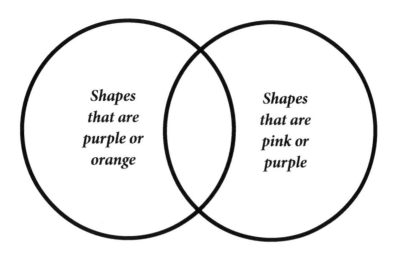

Shapes that are purple or orange

Shapes that are pink or purple

Which shape would belong in the area where the two circles overlap?
(A) a pink square
(B) a purple rectangle
(C) an orange triangle
(D) a pink circle

6. Brett polled his classmates about their favorite types of dinner. He made a circle graph from their answers.

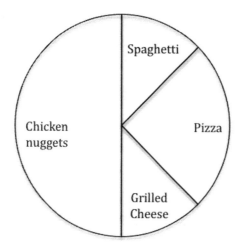

Roughly what fraction of Brett's classmates chose grilled cheese as their favorite type of dinner?

(A) $\frac{1}{8}$

(B) $\frac{1}{6}$

(C) $\frac{1}{4}$

(D) $\frac{1}{2}$

7. Sarah wrote her classmates names on cards and then put them in a hat. The chance that she will randomly pick a card with a girls name on it from the hat is 4 out of 7. There are 16 girls in the class. How many boys are there?

(A) 9

(B) 10

(C) 12

(D) 28

8. The graph below shows number of pairs of eyeglasses sold in the month of March at various stores.

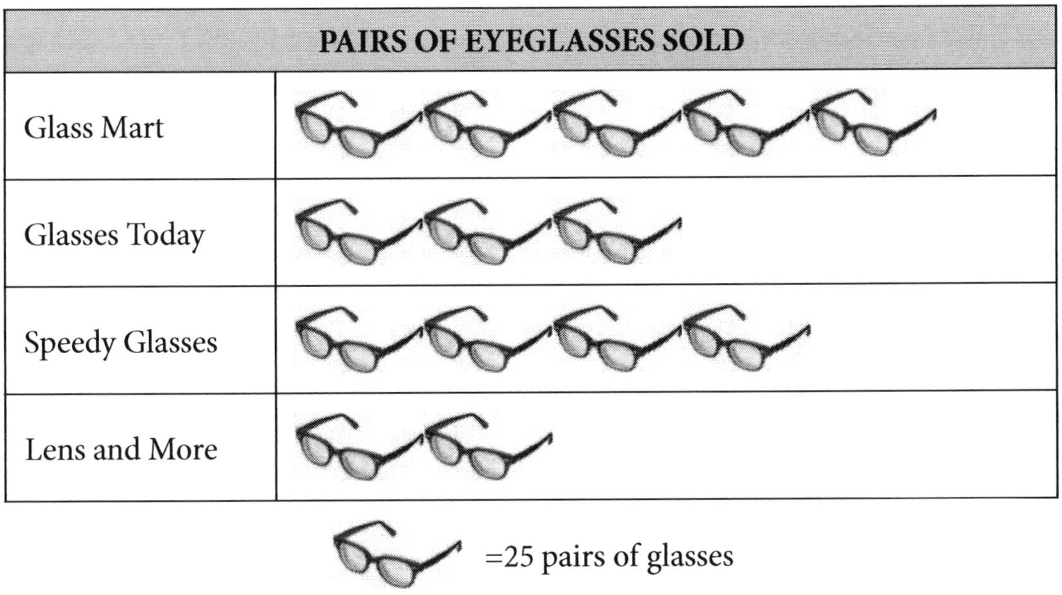

PAIRS OF EYEGLASSES SOLD

Glass Mart	
Glasses Today	
Speedy Glasses	
Lens and More	

=25 pairs of glasses

How many more pairs of glasses did Glass Mart sell compared to Lens and More?
(A) 3
(B) 5
(C) 50
(D) 75

9. For five days, Jake recorded the number of airplanes that he saw flying over his house. He recorded his data below.

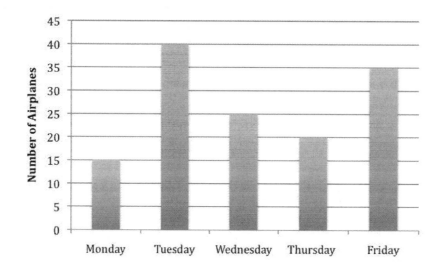

Based on the above graph, which conclusion is correct about the number of airplanes that Jake saw each day?

(A) The mean is between 28 and 30.

(B) The range is equal to the number of planes that Jake saw on Wednesday.

(C) Jake saw more planes on Tuesday than he saw on Monday and Wednesday combined.

(D) Jake saw more planes on Friday than on any other day.

10. Trey has a bag of markers that are different colors: green, yellow, red, blue, and black. The probability that he will randomly select a green marker is 3 out of 11. What is a possible combination of the markers in the bag?

(A) 3 green marker and 11 other markers

(B) 9 green markers and 11 other markers

(C) 9 green markers and 24 other markers

(D) 12 green markers and 15 other markers

Answers to probability and data practice set

1. B
2. D
3. C
4. A
5. B
6. A
7. C
8. D
9. B
10. C

Geometry

On the Lower Level ISEE, the geometry questions are pretty basic.

You will need to be able to:

- Define basic shapes
- Visualize how shapes fit together or could be divided
- Apply the concepts of symmetry, congruency, and similarity
- Understand how the coordinate system works
- Perform transformations

Define basic shapes

On the Lower Level ISEE, you will need to know the definitions of various shapes. In general, we can divide the shapes into quadrilaterals and not quadrilaterals.

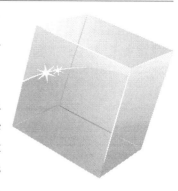

Quadrilaterals are simply shapes that have four sides. A shape can also be described by more than one name. For example, a square is also a rectangle, a parallelogram, and a quadrilateral. The least specific name for a square is a quadrilateral since that just tells us that has four sides. A little more specific is the name parallelogram, which tells us that it has two pairs of parallel sides. Even more specific is the term rectangle. Now we know that not only does the figure have two pairs of parallel sides, but also that all of the figure's angles are right angles. Finally, the most specific name is square- telling us that the figure has four sides, all the angles are right angles, and all the sides are of the same length.

- Quadrilaterals are shapes with four sides
- A shape can have more than one name

The quadrilaterals that you will need to know for the Lower Level ISEE include:

- Parallelogram
- Rectangle
- Square
- Kite
- Rhombus
- Diamond
- Trapezoid

A parallelogram is a shape with two pairs of parallel lines and opposite sides that are the same length.

Here is an example of a parallelogram:

A rectangle is a parallelogram that has four right angles. Here is an example of a rectangle:

Finally, a square is a rectangle that has four sides of the same length. Here is an example of a square:

Another type of quadrilateral is a kite. A kite is a four-sided shape that has two pairs of adjacent sides that are the same length. (adjacent means that the sides are next to each other). Here is an example of a kite:

A special kind of kite is a rhombus. A rhombus has four sides that are all the same length. A rhombus can also be called a diamond. Here is an example of a rhombus or diamond:

A rhombus can also have four right angles- in this case the more specific name for that shape would be square.

The final type of quadrilateral that you may see is a trapezoid. A trapezoid has one set of opposite, parallel sides and one set of adjacent acute angles (less than 90 degrees) and one set of adjacent obtuse angles (more than 90 degrees). Here is an example of a trapezoid:

You will also need to know some shapes that are not quadrilaterals. These shapes include:

- Triangles
- Pentagons
- Hexagons

Triangles are simply shapes that have three sides. Here is an example:

A pentagon is a shape that has five sides. Here is an example of a pentagon:

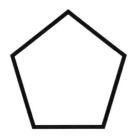

Finally, you need to know that a hexagon has six sides. Here is an example of a hexagon:

Below are some sample questions that test these definitions. On the ISEE, you are more likely to see a coordinate geometry question that also tests the definitions of shapes, so we will have more of those in the coordinate geometry section.

Here are some questions for you to try:

1. What is the name of a shape that has six sides?
    (A) pentagon
    (B) hexagon
    (C) trapezoid
    (D) triangle

A shape that has six sides is a hexagon. The prefix "hex" means six, so any shape with six sides is a hexagon. Answer choice B is correct.

2. What name best describes a rhombus with four right angles?
    (A) square
    (B) diamond
    (C) trapezoid
    (D) pentagon

If we go to the answer choices, we can rule out choices C and D right away because neither a trapezoid nor a pentagon has four right angles. Now we are left with choices A and B. This is tricky because a rhombus can also be a diamond or a square. However, while a diamond can have right angles, it does not have to. A square must have right angles, however, so answer choice A is correct.

You will also need to know a couple of basic three-dimensional shapes. The previous shapes were two-dimensional in that they had length and width and lay flat in a plane. Three-dimensional figures also have height.

- Three-dimensional figures also have height

For the Lower Level ISEE, you have to know what a rectangular prism is. A rectangular prism is basically the same shape as a cardboard box. It is made up of six rectangles. A special kind of rectangular prism is a cube. A cube is a rectangular prism with side lengths that are all equal.

- Think of a rectangular prism as being the shape of a box
- A cube is a rectangular prism with side lengths that are equal

Generally, the Lower Level ISEE will not ask you to define a prism or cube. Rather they will ask you to apply the concepts. These question types show up in the measurement section of this book, so for now just tuck away the definitions to use later.

Visualize how shapes fit together or could be divided

Some questions will ask you to picture the different ways you could divide a figure or how two pieces would fit together.

The trick to these questions is to use your pencil to draw out the possibilities.

- Use your pencil to draw it out

For questions that ask you to divide a figure, most often the question will ask you how many triangular regions can be created. A triangular region is just a region that has three sides. You may also see the word vertex (the plural is vertices), which is just a "corner" of a figure, or where two sides come together.

- A triangular region is just a region with three sides
- A vertex (plural: vertices) is the point where two sides meet

Here are a couple of examples of questions that ask you to divide a figure:

1. Use the figure below to answer the question.

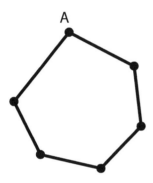

Harold draws lines connecting the vertex A to each of the other vertices. How many triangular regions can he create?

(A) 3
(B) 4
(C) 5
(D) 6

Let's go ahead and draw in those lines. Now our picture looks like this:

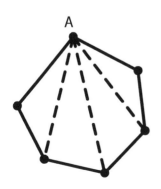

If we count up the triangular regions, it is clear that Harold can create four triangular regions. Answer choice B is correct.

2. Hannah is dividing her garden into triangular regions. She has put stakes in the ground at points A, B, C, D, and E. She put a string around the perimeter of these stakes as shown.

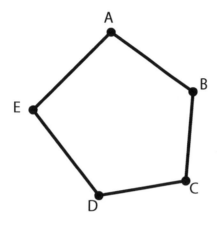

Hannah is going to use string to connect stake A to each of the other stakes. How many triangular regions can she create?

(A) 2

(B) 3

(C) 4

(D) 5

Again, we will draw it out. Our picture should look like this:

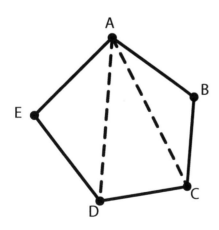

Now we can see that Hannah could create 3 triangular regions. Answer choice B is correct.

Here is an example of a question that asks you to picture how pieces could fit together:

3. The diagram below was created by putting several small squares together.

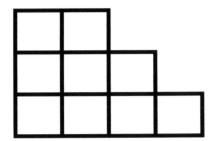

Which piece would complete the diagram to create one larger square?

(A)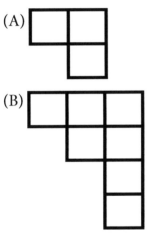

(B)

(C)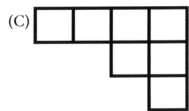

(D)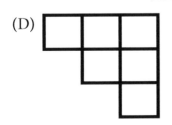

The trick to this question is to recognize that in order to make a perfect square, the figure must be four squares high since it is four squares wide. That means that we must add three squares to the height on the right side of the figure. This allows us to eliminate choices A and B. We can also see that we must add a full row of four squares across the top. Since choice D has only three squares across the top, we can eliminate choice D. Answer choice C is correct.

Symmetry, congruency, and similarity

On the Lower Level ISEE, you will need to know what the terms symmetric, congruent, and similar mean.

- Symmetric- a shape is symmetric if you could draw a line down the middle and the two halves would be flipped versions of each other.

Here is an example:

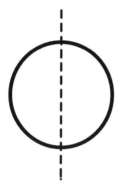 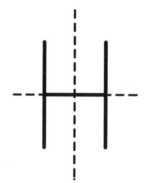

A circle is symmetric because if we folded it along the dotted line, the two sides awould match up. A circle has many lines of symmetry since we could draw that dotted line in many places and still have the two halves match up.

The letter H above has two lines of symmetry. The two dashed lines show the lines of symmetry.

The letter Z above doesn't have any lines of symmetry. We cannot draw any lines that make the two sides match up exactly.

- Congruent- two objects are congruent if they are the same length/size/shape.

Here is an example:

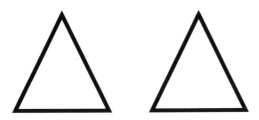

The two triangles above are congruent because they are exactly the same size and shape.

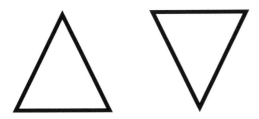

The two triangles above are also congruent. Even though one triangle has been flipped, they are still the same size and shape so they are congruent.

- Similar- two shapes are similar if they have the same angles and side lengths that are in proportion to one another.

Here is an example:

The two triangles above are similar because they have the same angle measures and each side of the smaller triangle is half the length of the corresponding side of the larger triangle.

Here are some examples of questions that test these concepts:

1. Which figure below has exactly two lines of symmetry?

(A)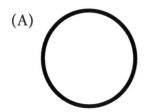

(B)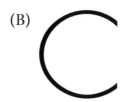

(C)

(D)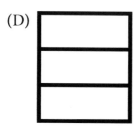

We are looking for a figure that we could fold in two different ways and have the sides match up. The figure in answer A has infinite lines of symmetry since you could draw many lines and have the sides match up. We can rule out choice A. Answer choice B has only one line of symmetry. We could draw a line across the letter C and have the top and bottom halves match up, but there isn't a second line of symmetry. Answer choice B can be eliminated. In answer choice C, the letter N has no lines of symmetry. Answer choice C can be ruled out. Finally, we have answer choice D. We could draw a line across the middle of the figure and the top and bottom halves would match up. We could also draw a line up and down on the figure and the right and left halves would match up. Answer choice D is correct.

2. The figure below could be folded along the dotted lines.

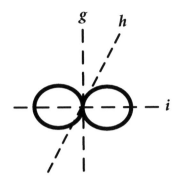

Which line (or pair of lines), when folded, would allow the two halves of the figure to match up exactly?
(A) line *g* only
(B) line *h* only
(C) lines *g* and *h*
(D) lines *g* and *i*

This question doesn't use the word "symmetric", but that is what the question is really testing. We are looking for which lines are lines of symmetry for the figure. Only lines *g* and *i* would cause the two halves to match up, so answer choice D is the correct answer.

3. Which pair of figures below is congruent?

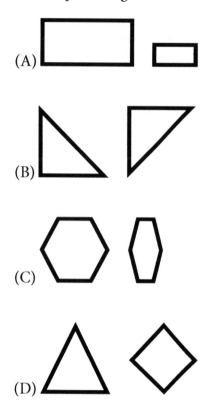

(A)

(B)

(C)

(D)

We are looking for two figures that are exactly the same. In choice A, the two figures are similar, but not congruent. Choice A can be ruled out. Choice B has two figures that are exactly the same. One figure is rotated, but the two triangles still have the same angles and the same side lengths, so they are congruent. Answer choice B is the correct choice.

4. Use the figure below to answer the question.

Which figure is similar to the triangle above?

(A)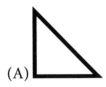

(B)

(C)

(D)

We are looking for a figure that is a triangle with the same angle measures as the given triangle. Answer choices B and D aren't even triangles, so we can eliminate those answer choices. Answer choice A is a triangle, but we don't want a right triangle so choice A can be eliminated. Choice C is the correct answer.

Coordinate geometry

Coordinate geometry uses a grid. The important thing to remember about points on a coordinate grid is that the x-coordinate is given first and then the y-coordinate. Ordered pairs are written (x,y). If you have trouble remembering what comes first, just think "first you run, then you jump".

Here is an example:

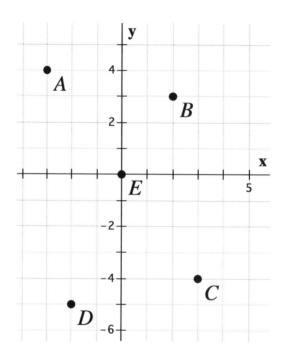

In the coordinate grid above, there are several points plotted.

On this grid, we would call point E the origin. The coordinates of point E are $(0, 0)$.

The coordinates of point B are $(2, 3)$ because we go over 2 and up 3 to get to point B from the origin.

If we have to go to the left of the origin, then the x-coordinate becomes a negative number. If we have to go down (instead of up), then the y-coordinate is negative.

Therefore, the coordinates of point A are $(-3, 4)$.

What are the coordinates of point D?

We would have to go the left two spots to get from the origin to point *D*, so the x-coordinate is −2. We would then have to go down 5 places, so the y-coordinate of point *D* is −5. We would write to coordinates of point *D* as (−2, −5).

What about point *C*?

Let's remember to run then jump. To get from the origin to point *C*, we would have go 3 places to the right in the positive direction and then go down 4 places in the negative direction. The coordinates of point *C* are (3, −4).

Here is an example of a question that tests the coordinate grid on the Lower Level ISEE:

1. Use the coordinate grid below to answer the question.

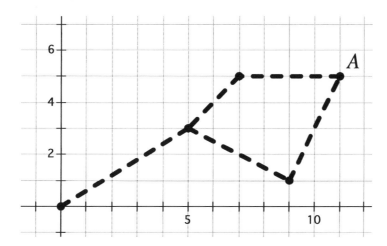

What are the (*x*, *y*) coordinates of point *A* in the figure above?
(A) (9, 5)
(B) (11, 5)
(C) (5, 11)
(D) (5, 9)

To get from the origin to point *A*, we have to go over 11 spaces and then up 5 spaces. This means the coordinates of point *A* are (11, 5). Answer choice B is correct.

Some of the questions on the ISEE that test coordinate geometry also test the definition of shapes.

Here are a couple of examples for you to try:

2. Jackie plots the points (1, 2), (2, 3), (4, 3), and (5, 2). She then connects these points to make a quadrilateral. Which term could describe that quadrilateral?
(A) square
(B) diamond
(C) hexagon
(D) trapezoid

The best way to answer this question is to draw our own grid. It does not have to be exact since we are just looking for a rough idea of where the points are in relation to one another.

Your grid should look something like this:

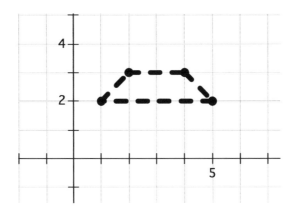

We can see that the shape is clearly not a square or a diamond, so we can rule out choices A and B. Choice C, a hexagon, is not even a quadrilateral so it can be eliminated. Answer choice D is the correct answer.

3. The vertices of a quadrilateral are (2, 2), (4, 0), (6, 2), and (4, 4). Which term best describes this quadrilateral?
(A) pentagon
(B) square
(C) trapezoid
(D) hexagon

Again, let's plot the points and see what we have. Our grid looks something like this when we plot the points and then connect them:

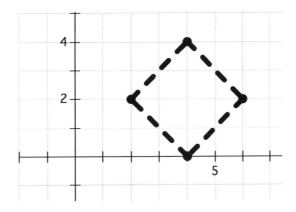

Even though the shape is turned diagonally on the axes, it is still definitely a square. It has four sides that are the same length and four right angles. Answer choice B is correct.

Transformations

A transformation is basically just moving or flipping a figure. In order for it to be a transformation, the side lengths and angles must remain unchanged.

- A transformation moves a figure but does not change the figure itself

There are three main types of transformations:

1. Rotation or turn- in this transformation, a figure is just turned.

Here is an example:

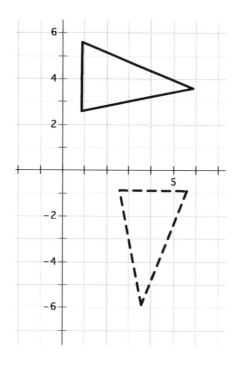

The solid figure is just rotated, or turned, but notice that it is still the same figure.

2. Reflection or flip- with this transformation, a figure is flipped across a line. The line that the figure is flipped across is often the x-axis or the y-axis.

Here is an example:

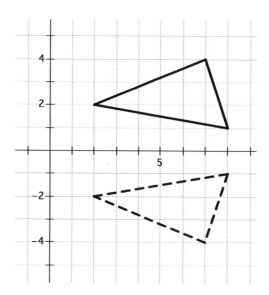

The figure with solid lines has been reflected across the x-axis to create the figure with dashed lines.

3. Translation or slide- in this transformation the figure is not turned or reflected, but rather just slid to a new location.

Here is an example:

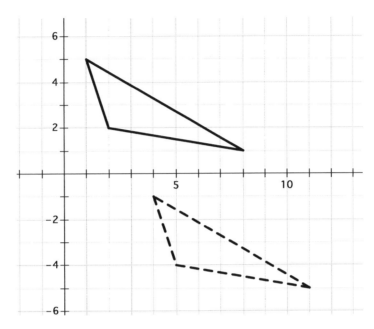

In the above figure, the solid line triangle has just been slid down and to the right to create the dashed line triangle.

Here are two examples of questions that test transformations:

1. Use the coordinate grid below to answer the question.

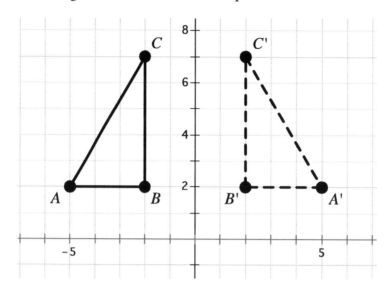

Which transformation took place with triangle *ABC* to get triangle *A'B'C'*?
(A) a slide
(B) a flip
(C) a flip and then another flip
(D) a turn

Triangle *ABC* is the mirror image of triangle *A'B'C'*. This means that a flip, or reflection, must have occurred. This allows us to rule out answer choices A and D. Triangle *ABC* was only flipped once to get *A'B'C'*, so answer choice B is correct.

2. Use the coordinate grid below to answer the question.

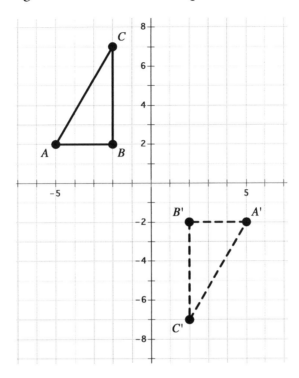

What transformation must have been applied to triangle *ABC* in order to get triangle *A'B'C'*?

(A) a flip only

(B) a slide only

(C) a flip and then another flip

(D) a slide and then a flip

Let's use ruling out on this question. If only a flip was applied, then triangle *A'B'C'* would be in either the top right or bottom left quadrant. This is not the case, so we can rule out choice A. If only a slide was applied to triangle *ABC* then point C would still be at the top of the figure. It is not, so we can rule out choice B. If triangle *ABC* was flipped over the y–axis and then flipped over the x–axis, triangle *A'B'C'* would be the result. Answer choice C is correct.

Those are the basics that you need to know for geometry questions on the Lower Level ISEE. Be sure to complete the geometry practice set to reinforce what you have learned.

Geometry practice set

1. The coordinate points (2, 6), (3, 8), (4, 6), and (3,1) are connected to form a quadrilateral. What term would best describe this quadrilateral?
   (A) square
   (B) kite
   (C) trapezoid
   (D) rhombus

2. Which pair below has two figures that are similar?

(A)

(B)

(C)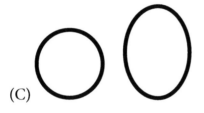

(D)

3. Use the coordinate grid below to answer the question.

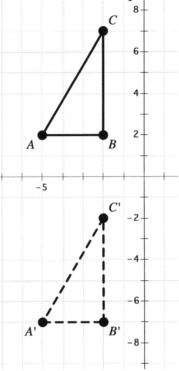

Which transformation could be applied to triangle *ABC* to get triangle *A'B'C'*?
(A) a flip only
(B) a flip and then a slide
(C) a slide only
(D) a turn

4. Which figure always has sides that are all the same length?
(A) rhombus
(B) pentagon
(C) hexagon
(D) rectangle

5. Use the coordinate grid below.

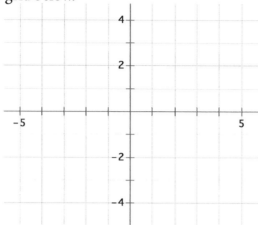

Craig plotted the points (2, 2), (−2, 2), (−2, −2), and (2, −2) on the coordinate grid. He then connected the points to form a polygon. What kind of polygon did he form?

(A) rectangle

(B) pentagon

(C) triangle

(D) trapezoid

6. Use the diagram below to answer the question.

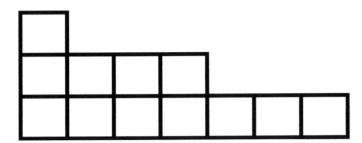

Which piece could be used to complete the diagram and create a rectangle?

(A)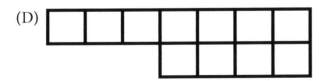

(B)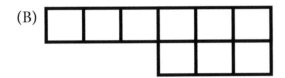

(C)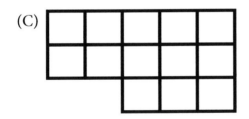

(D)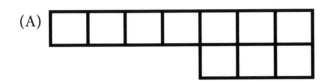

7. Use the coordinate grid below to answer the question.

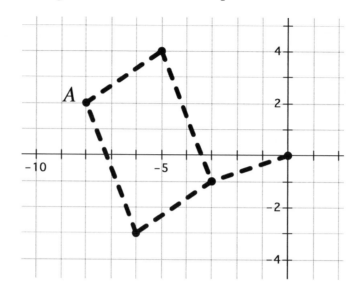

What are the (x, y) coordinates of point A?
(A) (8, –2)
(B) (–2, 8)
(C) (2, –8)
(D) (–8, 2)

8. Use the diagram below to answer the question.

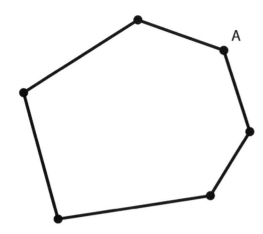

Valerie drew lines to connect point *A* to each of the other vertices. How many triangular regions did she create?

(A) 2

(B) 3

(C) 4

(D) 5

9. Which pair below has two figures with the same number of lines of symmetry?

(A)

(B)

(C)

(D)

10. What is another name for a quadrilateral that has two pairs of opposite parallel sides?
    (A) parallelogram
    (B) kite
    (C) trapezoid
    (D) pentagon

Answers to geometry practice set

1. B
2. D
3. C
4. A
5. A
6. B
7. D
8. C
9. B
10. A

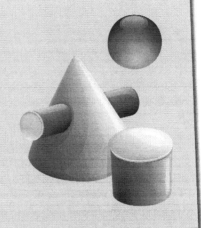

Measurement

On the Lower Level ISEE, there are just a few measurement concepts that you need to know. They include:

- Perimeter
- Area
- Volume of rectangular solids
- What units to use when
- How to convert units
- How to convert time zones

Perimeter

Perimeter is defined as the distance around a figure. To find the perimeter of a figure, just add up the side lengths.

- *Perimeter = side + side + side...*

Some questions are very straightforward and just ask you to add up the sides to find the perimeter.

Here are some examples:

1. Use the triangle below to answer the question.

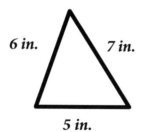

What is the perimeter of this triangle?
$(P = s + s + s)$
(A) 16 in.
(B) 18 in.
(C) 22 in.
(D) 34 in.

To find the perimeter, we just add up the side lengths: $6 + 7 + 5 = 18$. Answer choice B is correct.

2. What is the perimeter of a rectangle that has a width of 4 inches and a length of 6 inches?
$(P = 2l + 2w)$
(A) 10 inches
(B) 14 inches
(C) 16 inches
(D) 20 inches

To find the perimeter, we just plug into the equation that the question gives us: $P = 2l + 2w = 2(6) + 2(4) = 12 + 8 = 20$. Answer choice D is correct.

3. Tara is going to build a rectangular garden as shown below.

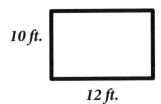

10 ft.

12 ft.

She wants to run a string around the perimeter of the garden. How many feet of string will she need of string to go all the way around her garden?
(A) 20 ft.
(B) 22 ft.
(C) 42 ft.
(D) 44 ft.

In order to figure out how much string Tara will need, we need to find the perimeter of the garden. To do that, we add up the lengths of the sides. The key is to remember to add two lengths and two widths. If we add $10 + 10 + 12 + 12$, we get that the perimeter of Tara's garden is 44 ft., so she will need 44 ft. of string. Answer choice D is correct.

Some questions will give you the perimeter and then ask you to work backwards to solve for a side length.

Here are a couple of examples:

4. Use the triangle below to answer the question.

If the perimeter of the triangle is 22 cm, then what is the length of the third side?
(A) 10 cm
(B) 12 cm
(C) 22 cm
(D) 34 cm

For this question, we need to first add up the lengths of the sides that we do have: 5 *cm*+7 *cm* = 12 *cm*. Now we subtract that sum from the total perimeter to figure out the length of the third side: 22 *cm* −12 *cm* = 10 *cm*. Answer choice A is correct.

5. If the perimeter of a square is 12*w*, then what is the length of one side?
(A) 3
(B) 4
(C) 3*w*
(D) 4*w*

The trick to this question is to not forget the *w*. Since perimeter of a square is equal to 4 × *side length*, we know that we must divide the perimeter by 4 in order to get the side length. If we divide 12*w* by 4, we get 3*w*. Answer choice C is correct.

Area

Area is the surface that a figure takes up or the amount of space inside a figure.

On the Lower Level ISEE, you will need know how to find the area of a rectangle and the area of a triangle.

Area of a rectangle = length × width

Area of a triangle = $\frac{1}{2}$ × base × height

For example, let's say we have to find the area of the rectangle below:

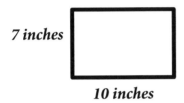

7 inches

10 inches

Area of a rectangle = length × width = 7 in. × 10 in. = 70 in.²

Notice that the units that describe area are squared.

Keep in mind that a square is also a rectangle. This means that the area of a square is also length × width. Since length and width are the same with a square, you will generally just be given one side length.

For example, let's say we need to find the area of the square below:

5

We still do length × width, we just plug in the number 5 for both the length and the width.

Area of a rectangle = length × width = 5 in. × 5 in. = 25 in.²

On the Lower Level ISEE, you will generally be asked to find the area of right triangles, or triangles that have one angle that is 90 degrees.

The area of a triangle is found by using the formula:

$$Area\ of\ a\ triangle = \tfrac{1}{2} \times base \times height$$

For example, let's say that you want to find the area of the following triangle:

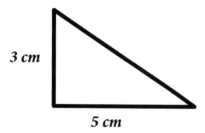

3 cm

5 cm

We just need to plug into the formula:

$$Area\ of\ a\ triangle = \tfrac{1}{2} \times base \times height = \tfrac{1}{2} \times 3\ cm \times 5\ cm = 7\tfrac{1}{2}\ cm^2$$

Notice that since we found an area, the units are squared.

On the Lower Level ISEE, more often than not area problems require you to divide a figure into pieces, find the area of each piece, and then add those areas together.

For example, let's say that we have to find the area of the figure below:

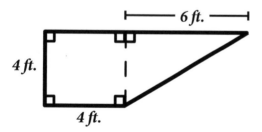

6 ft.

4 ft.

4 ft.

To find the area of the entire figure, we first have to divide it into pieces. We have a square on the left side and a triangle on the right side.

The area of the square is: $4 \times 4 = 16$ sq. ft.

The area of the triangle is: $\tfrac{1}{2}(4 \times 6) = 12$ sq. ft. (We had to use the fact that all sides of a square are the same length in order to get the height of the triangle).

Now we add the areas of those two regions together in order to get the area of the entire figure:

Area $= 16\ sq.\ ft. + 12\ sq.\ ft. = 28\ sq.\ ft.$

Here are a couple of examples of questions that test this concept:

1. Hillside Elementary is planning to build a new garden. The garden plan is shown below.

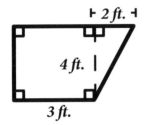

According to the garden plan, what is the area of the garden?
(A) 4 sq. ft.
(B) 10 sq. ft.
(C) 12 sq. ft.
(D) 16 sq. ft.

First, we have to find the area of the rectangle:

Area of a rectangle $= l \times w = 4 \times 3 = 12\ sq.\ ft.$

Now we have to find the area of the triangle:

$\frac{1}{2}(b \times h) = \frac{1}{2}(2 \times 4) = \frac{1}{2}(8) = 4\ sq.\ ft.$

To find the total area, we just have to add the area of the rectangle and the area of the triangle:

total area $= 4\ sq.\ ft. + 12\ sq.\ ft. = 16\ sq.\ ft.$

Answer choice D is the correct answer.

2. The figure below was created by combining a square with two congruent triangles.

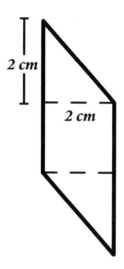

What is the total area of the figure?
(A) 2 cm^2
(B) 4 cm^2
(C) 8 cm^2
(D) 12 cm^2

The question tells us that the figure is made up of a square and two triangles. That is a good indicator that we should find the area of a square and two triangles!

Area of a square = side × side = 2 × 2 = 4 cm²

Area of one triangle = $\frac{1}{2}(b × h) = \frac{1}{2}(2 × 2) = \frac{1}{2}(4) = 2$ cm²

Area of two triangles = 2 × 2 cm² = 4 cm²

Total area = area of square + area of triangles = 4 + 4 = 8cm²

Answer choice C is correct.

Another type of area question requires you to find the area of a portion of a figure (usually you are looking for the area of a shaded region).

The trick to these questions is that you have to first find the area of the bigger figure and then subtract off smaller shapes.

- For these "shaded portion" questions, you have to find the area of a bigger figure and then subtract to find the shaded area

Here are a couple of examples:

3. Figure 1 below is a rectangle. Four congruent triangles are removed from the corners of Figure 1 in order to create Figure 2, as shown below.

Figure 1

Figure 2

What is the area of Figure 2?
(A) 2 in^2
(B) 4 in^2
(C) 6 in^2
(D) 8 in^2

Our first step is to find the area of the bigger figure:

Area of a rectangle = l × w = 4 × 2 = 8 in²

Now we have to find the area of the triangles that are cut out:

Area of one triangle = ½(b × h) = ½(2 × 1) = ½(2) = 1 in²

Area of 4 triangles = 4 × 1 in² = 4 in²

Now we subtract the triangles from the bigger figure:

Area of rectangle − Area of triangles = 8 in² − 4 in² = 4 in²

The correct answer is choice B.

4. The large square shown below has four smaller squares within it. Half of each of these squares is shaded.

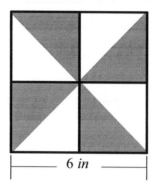

6 in

What is the area of the shaded region?
(A) 18 in^2
(B) 24 in^2
(C) 36 in^2
(D) 48 in^2

First we need to find the area of the bigger square. Since each side of the bigger square is 6 *in.*, the area of the larger square is 36 in^2. Now, we just have to find half the area of the larger square. Even though it does not tell us that half of the square is shaded, it does tell us that half of the regions that make up the larger square are shaded. Since 36 in^2 ÷ 2 = 18 in^2, answer choice A is correct.

Some questions may give you an area and ask you which dimensions would create that area. For these questions, you just have to try out the answer choices and see what works since there are multiple pairs of dimensions that give the same area.

•   If the question gives you an area and asks for dimensions, just try out the answer choices

Here is an example of this type of question:

5.   A rectangle has an area of 42 cm². What could be the dimensions of this rectangle?
(A) 2 *cm* × 22 *cm*
(B) 3 *cm* × 14 *cm*
(C) 4 *cm* × 16 *cm*
(C) 6 *cm* × 8 *cm*

Let's go ahead and figure out the area of each answer choice!

      (A) $2\ cm \times 22\ cm = 44\ cm^2$
      (B) $3\ cm \times 14\ cm = 42\ cm^2$
      (C) $4\ cm \times 16\ cm = 64\ cm^2$
      (D) $6\ cm \times 8\ cm = 48\ cm^2$

We can see that only the dimensions given in answer choice B create a rectangle with an area of $42\ cm^2$. Answer choice B is correct.

Some other questions may ask you to find the area of a shape that is placed over a coordinate grid. To answer these questions, generally you can just count up how many squares the figure covers. You will have to estimate if you do this since some of the squares will be only partially covered. The other way to answer these questions is to divide the figure into pieces, find the area of each piece, and then add those areas together to get the total.

- If a figure is placed over a coordinate grid you can count up how many squares are covered but remember to estimate and not count partially covered squares as full squares

Here is an example of this type of question:

6. Use the coordinate grid below to answer the question.

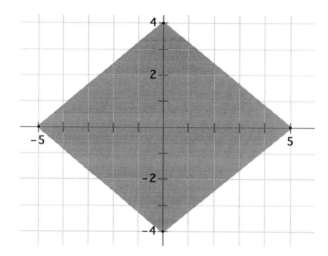

What is the area of the rhombus in the figure above?
(A) 30
(B) 35
(C) 40
(D) 45

To answer this question, we can count up how many squares are covered, estimating for squares that are not completely covered by the rhombus. Since this is a multiple-choice test, we can come close enough using this method to get the right answer. Another option, however, is to divide the figure into four smaller triangles. We can use the numbers on the axes to figure out that each triangle is 4 units high and 5 units across.

Now we can use our area formula:

Area of one triangle $= \frac{1}{2}(b \times h) = \frac{1}{2}(4 \times 5) = \frac{1}{2}(20) = 10$

Area of four triangles $= 10 \times 4 = 40$

Answer choice C is correct.

Volume of rectangular solids

On the Lower Level ISEE, you may see questions that ask you about the volume of rectangular prisms. Think of a rectangular prism as being the shape of a cardboard box. A cube is just a rectangular prism that has sides that are all the same length.

- Think of a rectangular prism as being the shape of the cardboard box with the lid on
- A cube is a rectangular prism with side lengths that are all equal- picture dice

The volume of a rectangular prism (or cube) is just:

volume = length × width × height

Since a rectangular prism is a 3-D (short for three-dimensional) figure, we have to multiply all three dimensions to find the volume.

A basic question will just ask you to figure out the dimensions. It is important to remember how 3-D representations work. With a 3-D picture, you can't see all of the figure. Rectangular prism questions often ask you to divide a larger prism into smaller cubes and you have to remember that there are cubes that you cannot see.

- Remember that with a 3-D picture, we cannot see the entire figure

Here is an example of some rectangular prism questions:

1. The prism below was built by stacking one-unit cubes.

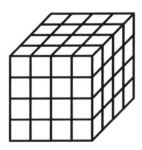

Which computation correctly shows how the volume of the larger prism could be found?
(A) 4 × 4 × 4 × 2
(B) 4 × 4 × 16
(C) 4 × 4 × 4
(D) 16 × 16 × 16

To answer this question, we first have to figure out the dimensions. From the face of the prism, we can see that the length is 4 units and the height is also 4 units. If we count back, we can see that the width is also 4 units (see diagram below).

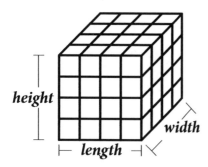

The volume of the prism would therefore be found by multiplying 4 by 4 by 4. Answer choice C is correct.

2. Use the diagram below to answer the question.

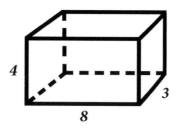

What is the volume of the prism above, in cubic units?
(A) 48
(B) 96
(C) 120
(D) 144

To find the volume of a prism, we have to multiply *length × width × height*. We can plug the dimensions that are given into this equation and get:

length × width × height = 8 × 3 × 4 = 96 *cubic units*

Answer choice B is the correct answer.

3. Use the figure below to answer the question.

How many smaller cubes were used to build the larger cube?
(A) 9
(B) 18
(C) 27
(D) 36

This is really just a volume question even though it does not use the word "volume" at all. We can see that the front face of the larger cube has dimensions of 3 × 3. We can also see that the prism is three cubes deep. If we multiply 3 × 3 × 3, we get that there must have been 27 smaller cubes used to build the bigger cube. Answer choice C is correct.

The following question is a little different, but just use the same principles. If it makes it easier, you can also create your own sketch.

4. The small cube below is 1 inch on all sides. How many cubes of this size would be required to create a larger cube that is 2 inches on all sides?

(A) 2
(B) 4
(C) 8
(D) 16

One way to think of the problem is to compare the volumes of the two cubes. The volume of the small cube is $1 \times 1 \times 1 = 1 \ in^3$. The volume of the 2-inch cube is $2 \times 2 \times 2 = 8 \ in^3$. The larger cube has 8 times the volume of the smaller cube, so we would need 8 of the smaller cubes to create a cube that is 2 inches on each side. Answer choice C is correct.

What units to use when

You may or may not see a question on the Lower Level ISEE that asks you what units to use for various measurements.

Units can be in either the English or the metric system.

Here is a basic chart of some units in the English system and what they measure:

What you want to measure	Units in the English system
Length	Inches, feet, and yards
Volume (or how much something can hold)	Cubic inches, cubic feet, and cubic yards for solid objects; for liquid we use tablespoons, cups, pints, quarts, and gallons
Weight (or mass)	Ounces and pounds

In the metric system, there are base units and then prefixes can be added. We won't spend a lot of time on this since you may not even see a units question on the Lower Level ISEE at all.

Here are the base units for the metric system:

What you want to measure	Base units in the metric system
Length	Meters
Volume (or how much something can hold)	Cubic meters for solid objects; for liquid we use liters
Weight (or mass)	Grams

If you do see a question about appropriate units on the Lower Level ISEE, here is what it could look like:

1. Laura is recording the volume of liquid that different jars can hold. What unit would be appropriate for her to use?
   (A) grams
   (B) inches
   (C) feet
   (D) cups

In this question, Laura is looking to record liquid volume. Inches and feet are both units of length, and not volume, so answer choices B and C can be eliminated. Grams is a measurement of how much something weighs and not how much it can hold, so answer choice A can be ruled out. Answer choice D is correct.

2. Paulo wants to measure a school bus. What would be the most appropriate units for him to use?
   (A) millimeters
   (B) centimeters
   (C) meters
   (D) kilometers

A school bus is pretty big, so it would take Paolo a long time to measure a school bus in either millimeters or centimeters. We can rule out answers A and B. A kilometer is much bigger than a school bus and there isn't a "kilometer" stick that he could use. We can eliminate choice D. Meters would be the most appropriate unit to use. Answer choice C is correct.

How to convert units

You may see a question on the Lower Level ISEE that asks you to convert between different units.

Some conversions that are good to know are:

60 *seconds* = 1 *minute*
60 *minutes* = 1 *hour*
24 *hours* = 1 *day*
12 *inches* = 1 *foot*
3 *feet* = 1 *yard*

Here are a couple of examples of questions that may ask you to convert between time units:

1. A song has a tempo of 2.5 beats per second. How many beats are there in one minute?
   (A) 60
   (B) 90
   (C) 120
   (D) 150

The question tells us that there are 2.5 beats in one second. There are 60 seconds in one minute, so we have to multiply 2.5 times 60 to get how many beats there are in a minute. Since $2.5 \times 60 = 150$, answer choice D is correct.

2. A machine stamps one envelope every 4 seconds. How many envelopes does the machine stamp in one minute?
   (A) 4
   (B) 15
   (C) 60
   (D) 240

The easiest way to answer this question is to set up a proportion. In order to set up a proportion, however, we need to have the same units on each side of the equal sign. We need to convert the one minute into 60 seconds.

$$\frac{1\ envelope}{4\ seconds} = \frac{n\ envelopes}{60\ seconds}$$

Now we can cross-multiply to solve.

$$1 \times 60 = 4 \times n$$
$$60 = 4n$$
$$\div 4 \quad \div 4$$
$$15 = n$$

The machine can stamp 15 envelopes in one minute, so answer choice B is correct.

Here are a couple of basic questions that ask you to convert between length units:

3. Sheila has a rope that is 2 feet 6 inches long. She needs to cut it into 3 equal pieces. How long should each piece be? Note: 1 foot = 12 inches
   (A) 5 inches
   (B) 6 inches
   (C) 10 inches
   (D) 12 inches

In order to divide the rope, we first have to convert 2 feet 6 inches into all inches.

Here is one way to think of this conversion:

2 feet 6 inches = 1 foot + 1 foot + 6 inches
= 12 inches + 12 inches + 6 inches
= 30 inches

Now that we know that the whole rope is 30 inches, it is easy to divide 30 by 3 and get that each piece must be 10 inches long. Answer choice C is correct.

4. Klaus wants to build a fence that is 36 feet long. The fencing comes in segments that are 1 yard long. How many segments will Klaus need? Note: 3 feet = 1 yard
   (A) 12
   (B) 15
   (C) 24
   (D) 36

To figure out how many segments are needed, we first need to convert the length of the fence into yards. We can use a proportion to do that:

$$\frac{3\ feet}{1\ yard} = \frac{36\ feet}{y\ yards}$$

Now we can cross-multiply:

$$3 \times y = 36 \times 1$$
$$3y = 36$$
$$y = 12$$

He needs 12 yards of fencing. Since each segment is one yard, Klaus would need 12 segments. The correct answer is choice A.

For questions that require you to convert between units of length and volume, the test question will generally give you the conversion.

One potential trick on conversion questions is that the conversions for length are NOT the same as the conversions for area.

For example, let's say that we have a rectangle that is 1 *ft.* × 1 *ft.*:

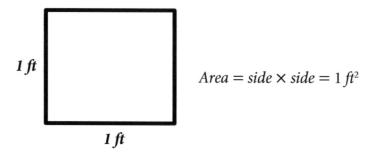

Now let's convert each side to inches. There are 12 inches in one foot, so each side is 12 inches long.

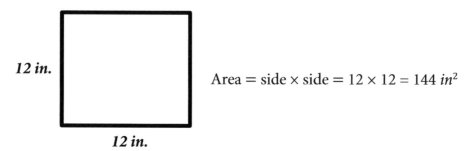

Notice that when we convert into inches, the area of the square is NOT 12 sq. inches. Rather, it is 144 sq. inches. The best way to handle these kinds of problems is to do conversions BEFORE you find the area.

- Do conversions BEFORE you find area

Here are a couple of questions that test finding area with conversions:

5. One gallon of paint will cover about 30 sq. yards of a wall. If Lisa wants to paint a wall that is 18 feet × 30 feet, how much paint will she need? Note: 1 yard = 3 feet.
   (A) 1
   (B) 2
   (C) 3
   (D) 4

First, we have to do our conversions:

$$18 \, feet \div 3 = 6 \, yards$$
$$30 \, feet \div 3 = 10 \, yards$$

Now we can find our area:

Area of a rectangle = length × width = 6 × 10 = 60 yd²

Since the area of the wall is 60 sq. yards and each gallon covers 30 sq. yards, we know that Lisa will need two gallons. Answer choice B is correct.

6. A family is planting a rectangular garden. They want to put 6 vegetable plants in each square yard. If their garden is 6 feet long and 12 feet wide, how many vegetable plants will they need? Note: 1 yard = 3 feet
   (A) 8
   (B) 24
   (C) 48
   (D) 72

Our first step is to convert the feet into yards. If you divide each dimension by 3 (since there are 3 feet in each yard), you get that the dimensions of the garden are *2 yards × 4 yards*. Now we have to multiply 2 by 4 to get that the area of the garden is 8 sq. yards. We don't have our answer yet, though, since there needs to be 6 plants per square yard. Since 8 times 6 is equal to 48, we know that they will need 48 plants. Answer choice C is correct.

How to convert time zones

You may see a question that asks you deal with different time zones. The trick to these questions is to keep all of the elements of the question in the same time zone.

- Convert all parts of the question into the same time zone

For example, when it is 9 AM in New York City (Eastern Standard Time), it is 6 AM in San Francisco (Pacific Standard Time).

A question might ask us if a flight took off in New York at 8 AM and landed in San Francisco five hours later, what would be the local time when the plane landed?

Let's put everything into Pacific Time to answer this question. If it was 8 AM in New York when the plane took off, it would have been 5 AM Pacific Time when the plane took off. Five hours later, it would have been 10 AM Pacific Time. Since we put everything into Pacific Time to begin with, it is easy to find that the local time was 10 AM Pacific Time when the plane landed.

Here is a question for you to try:

1. When it is 9 AM in Seattle, it is 12 PM in Philadelphia. An airplane leaves Seattle at 12 PM and lands in Philadelphia six hours later. What time is it in Philadelphia when the plane lands?
   (A) 6 AM
   (B) 12 PM
   (C) 6 PM
   (D) 9 PM

To answer this question, first we have to figure out what time it is in Philadelphia when the plane takes off. It is was 12 PM in Seattle, it would be 3 PM in Philadelphia. Six hours later, it would be 9 PM in Philadelphia. Answer choice D is correct.

Measurement practice set

1. Use the triangle below to answer the question.

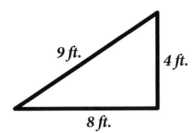

   What is the perimeter of this triangle?

   $P = s + s + s$

   (A) 21 feet
   (B) 24 feet
   (C) 30 feet
   (D) 32 feet

2. A rectangle has an area of 56 in^2. Which could be its dimensions?
   (A) 2 in × 24 in
   (B) 3 in × 16 in
   (C) 4 in × 12 in
   (D) 4 in × 14 in

3. Use the picture below to answer the question.

   How many smaller cubes were used to build the largest cube?
   (A) 9
   (B) 18
   (C) 27
   (D) 36

4. Myron is doing an experiment measuring how much a group of plants grows each day. Which would be an appropriate unit of measurement for him to use?
    (A) mile
    (B) inch
    (C) pound
    (D) liter

5. Carpet is $5 per square yard. Ms. Leonard wants to carpet a room that is 12 feet by 21 feet. How much will it cost her to carpet this room?
    (A) $70
    (B) $140
    (C) $200
    (D) $240

6. Use the diagram below to answer the question.

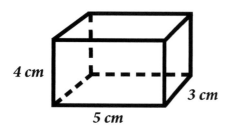

    What is the volume of the prism?
    (A) 12 cm^3
    (B) 20 cm^3
    (C) 30 cm^3
    (D) 60 cm^3

7. Quadrilateral *ABCD* is a square.

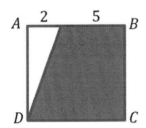

What is the area of the shaded region?
(A) 7
(B) 14
(C) 42
(D) 49

8. The perimeter of the triangle shown is 17cm.

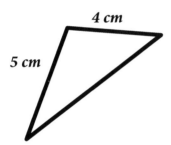

What is the length of the third side?
(A) 4 *cm*
(B) 5 *cm*
(C) 8 *cm*
(D) 9 *cm*

9. When it is 9 A.M. in New York City, it is 7 A.M. in Denver. An airplane leaves New York City at 1 P.M. and lands in Denver four hours later. What is the time in Denver when the plane lands?
(A) 3 P.M.
(B) 4 P.M.
(C) 5 P.M.
(D) 6 P.M.

10. A machine can print 10 brochures in one second. How many brochures can the machine print in one hour?

(A) 60

(B) 600

(C) 3,600

(D) 36,000

Answers to measurement practice set

1. A
2. D
3. C
4. B
5. B
6. D
7. C
8. C
9. A
10. D

Tips For the Writing Sample

When you take the ISEE, you will be asked to complete a writing sample at the very end of the test. You will be given 30 minutes and two pages to write your response.

You will also be given a piece of paper to take notes on.

- Writing sample is at the end of the test
- 30 minutes to complete
- Two pages to write on, plus one piece of paper for notes

Your writing sample will NOT be scored. Rather, a copy of it will be sent to the schools that you apply to. This essay is a great way for the admissions committee to get to know you better.

- Let your personality shine through so that admissions officers can get to know you better

You will be given a question to write from. The questions are topics that you can relate to your own life.

Here are some examples that are like the questions that you will see on the ISEE:

1. If you could change one thing about your school, what would it be? Why would you want to change it?
2. Who is your favorite teacher? Why did you choose this teacher?
3. If school was suddenly cancelled for the day, what would you do with your day? Describe in detail.

(There are more sample questions in ERB's official guide, *What to Expect on the ISEE*)

To approach the writing sample, follow this three-step plan

Step 1: Plan

- Take just a couple of minutes and plan, it will be time well spent
- Be sure to know what your main idea is and how each paragraph will be different
- Use the piece of paper provided

Step 2: Write

- Break your writing into paragraphs- don't do a two-page blob
- Write legibly- it does not have to be perfect and schools know that you are writing with a time limit, but if the admissions officers can't read what you wrote, they can't judge it
- Remember that each paragraph should have its own idea

Step 3: Edit/proofread

- Save a couple of minutes at the end to look over your work
- You won't be able to do a major editing job where you move around sentences and rewrite portions
- Look for where you may have left out a word or misspelled something
- Make your marks simple and clear- if you need to take something out, just put a single line through it and use a carat to insert words that you forgot

The writing sample is not graded, but the schools that you apply to do receive a copy.

What are schools looking for?

Organization

There should be structure to your essay. You need to have an introduction, good details to back up your main point, and a conclusion. Each paragraph should have its own idea.

Word choice

Use descriptive language. Don't describe anything as "nice" or "good". Describe specifically why something is nice or good. Good writing shows us and DOESN'T tell us.

Creativity and development of ideas

It is not enough just to be able to fit your writing into the form that you were taught in school. These prompts are designed to show how you think. This is your chance to shine!

The writing sample is a place for you to showcase your writing skills. It is just one more piece of information that the admissions committee will use in making their decisions.

The best way to get better at writing an essay is to practice. Try writing about one or more of the questions above. Use the prompts from *What to Expect on the ISEE*. Have a trusted adult help you analyze your writing sample and figure out how you can improve.

- Practice writing an essay before the actual test
- Have a teacher or parent help you analyze your practice essays

Practice Test

Following is a practice test for you to try. It is a full-length practice test with the same number of questions and timing as the actual test.

When you complete this practice test:

- Time yourself for each section
- Try to do the whole test in one sitting, if you can
- Check your answers and figure out WHY you missed the questions that you missed
- Keep in mind that the percentile charts are a very, very rough guideline- they are included just so you can see how the scoring works

There is additional practice available once you complete the practice test in this book. Test Prep Works has published another book, *The Best Unofficial Practice Tests for the Lower Level ISEE*, with two additional full-length practice tests. Also, be sure complete the practice test in *What to Expect on the ISEE* (available at www.erblearn.org). That will give you your best estimate of performance on the actual ISEE.

Section 1—Verbal Reasoning

34 questions

20 minutes

The Verbal Reasoning section has two parts. When you finish Part One, be sure to keep working on Part Two. For each answer that you choose, make sure to fill in the corresponding circle on the answer sheet.

Part One- Synonyms

The questions in Part One each have a word in all capital letters with four answer choices after it. Choose the answer choice with the word that comes closest in meaning to the word in all capital letters.

SAMPLE QUESTION:

1. SPEEDY:
   (A) loud
   (B) messy
   (●) quick
   (D) small

Part Two- Sentence Completions

The questions in Part Two each have a sentence with one blank. The blank takes the place of a word or phrase that is missing. The sentence has four answer choices after it. Choose the answer choice that would best complete the meaning of the sentence.

SAMPLE QUESTION:

1. Since the weather is getting warmer every day, it is particularly important to -------- more water.
   (A) create
   (●) drink
   (C) leave
   (D) waste

STOP. Do not move on to the section until told to.

Part One—Synonyms

Directions: Choose the word that is closest in meaning to the word that is in all capital letters.

1. OBJECTIVE
   (A) absence
   (B) editor
   (C) goal
   (D) rhyme

2. CURB
   (A) creak
   (B) glimpse
   (C) limit
   (D) proceed

3. HABITAT
   (A) application
   (B) decline
   (C) particle
   (D) residence

4. RESTORE
   (A) ditch
   (B) kneel
   (C) repair
   (D) review

5. TEMPERATE
   (A) familiar
   (B) mild
   (C) playful
   (D) silent

6. SACRED
   (A) holy
   (B) lingering
   (C) painful
   (D) rapid

Go on to the next page

7. PARTIAL
   (A) incomplete
   (B) local
   (C) prompt
   (D) relaxed

8. FORESHORTEN
   (A) accept
   (B) explain
   (C) neglect
   (D) reduce

9. OBEDIENTLY
   (A) drowsily
   (B) generally
   (C) respectfully
   (D) thankfully

10. COLLIDE
    (A) achieve
    (B) crash
    (C) muffle
    (D) wither

11. MAGNIFY
    (A) enlarge
    (B) hiss
    (C) plunge
    (D) strap

12. ABBREVIATE
    (A) badger
    (B) enliven
    (C) process
    (D) shorten

Go on to the next page

13. ENCLOSE
    (A) chirp
    (B) master
    (C) surround
    (D) worry

14. PLAYMATE
    (A) critic
    (B) friend
    (C) influence
    (D) transaction

15. PERSPECTIVE
    (A) disgust
    (B) occasion
    (C) reason
    (D) view

16. SERENE
    (A) calm
    (B) gaudy
    (C) jovial
    (D) prior

17. DRENCH
    (A) argue
    (B) fake
    (C) soak
    (D) toss

Go on to the next page

Part Two- Sentence Completions

Directions: Choose the word or phrase to best complete the sentence.

18. The unclear directions on the test left students ---------.
    (A) confident
    (B) inspired
    (C) perplexed
    (D) satisfied

19. Mice often choose ------ openings to get into a house such as cracks in a foundation or small gaps between the roof and the walls.
    (A) circular
    (B) narrow
    (C) personal
    (D) wide

20. Many companies try to conserve natural ------- such as water, clean air, and open space.
    (A) elevations
    (B) households
    (C) places
    (D) resources

21. Although no new monuments are currently being built in Rome, several have survived since the times of-------.
    (A) antiquity
    (B) drought
    (C) music
    (D) tomorrow

22. Christopher Columbus proved to be quite ------- when he set sail for the New World.
    (A) adventurous
    (B) lively
    (C) obedient
    (D) threatened

Go on to the next page

23. When sailors become ill on a ship, it is important that they are ------- before they infect other people on the ship.
    (A) admired
    (B) nominated
    (C) quarantined
    (D) veiled

24. Charles Dickens is known for creating characters with -----lives filled with misery and sorrow.
    (A) accomplished
    (B) favorable
    (C) original
    (D) wretched

25. Henry demonstrated his ------- when he visited several grocery stores to find the best price on eggs.
    (A) cheerfulness
    (B) frugality
    (C) jealousy
    (D) polish

26. Although the salesperson brought several dresses for Sheryl to try on, she was still --------.
    (A) dissatisfied
    (B) happy
    (C) mischievous
    (D) passive

27. The citizens united against the town's plan to close a park that was --------.
    (A) abominable
    (B) beloved
    (C) restless
    (D) temporary

Go on to the next page

28. Although the class was usually well-behaved with a substitute teacher, Ms. Myers got a report that her class' behavior was --------.
    (A) active
    (B) distinct
    (C) professional
    (D) unruly

29. Unlike many other writers who graduated from college, Ernest Hemingway-------.
    (A) was in the army
    (B) wrote seven novels
    (C) did not continue his formal education beyond high school
    (D) lived in Key West

30. Since her cat was howling at three in the morning, Carol --------.
    (A) went for a run
    (B) was tired the next day
    (C) bought more food
    (D) took her dog to the veterinarian

31. The purpose of the show was just to entertain the audience, and not to --------.
    (A) teach a lesson
    (B) provide enjoyment
    (C) make the time pass more quickly
    (D) provide amusement

32. Scientists once thought that all African elephants were the same species, but now -------.
    (A) the elephants are close to extinction
    (B) skeletons have been found of older elephants
    (C) many tourists come to see the elephants
    (D) there is evidence that there may be two species of African elephants

33. Although he was well-known as a musician during his lifetime, Johann Sebastian Bach was not known as a composer -------.
    (A) during his childhood
    (B) until after his death
    (C) in Europe
    (D) who wrote musical pieces

Go on to the next page

34. In contrast to countries near the Arctic Circle that experience harsh winters, the tropical country of Haiti -------.

(A) has many inhabitants
(B) is surrounded by water
(C) does not have snowstorms and ice in the winter
(D) has mild summers

STOP. If you have time left, you may check your answers in ONLY this section.

Section 2—Quantitative Reasoning

38 questions

35 minutes

Each math question has four answer choices after it. Choose the answer choice that best answers the question.

Make sure that you fill in the correct answer on your answer sheet. You may write in the test booklet.

SAMPLE QUESTION:

1. What is the perimeter of a rectangle that has a length of 3 cm and width of 5 cm?

    $(P = 2l + 2w)$

    (A) 6 cm
    (B) 10 cm
    (C) 8 cm
    (●) 16 cm

The correct answer is 16 cm and circle D is filled in.

STOP. Do not move on to the section until told to.

Section 2—Quantitative Reasoning

1. The square shown below is divided into smaller squares.

    What fraction of the largest square is shaded?
    (A) $\frac{4}{9}$
    (B) $\frac{4}{5}$
    (C) $\frac{1}{2}$
    (D) $\frac{2}{5}$

2. Which explanation best fits the following equation: $9 \div 3 = 3$?
    (A) I have 9 candies. If I give away 3 candies, how many do I have left?
    (B) I want to share 9 candies evenly with 3 friends. How many candies does each friend get?
    (C) I have 9 boxes of candy and each box has 3 candies in it. How many candies do I have all together?
    (D) I have 9 candies and my friend has 3 candies. How many candies do we have all together?

3. Carol hit more than 5 but less than 9 home runs. When John asked her how many home runs she hit, she told him that she had hit more than 7 but less than 11 home runs. How many home runs did Carol hit?
    (A) 6
    (B) 7
    (C) 8
    (D) 9

Go on to the next page

4. The triangle below has a perimeter of 35. Two of the side lengths are shown.

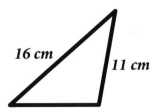

16 cm

11 cm

What is the length of the third side?
(A) 7 cm
(B) 8 cm
(C) 43 cm
(D) 46 cm

5. To answer the following question, use the equations below.

$4 + s = 7$
$5 + t = 7$

What is $s + t$ equal to?
(A) 1
(B) 3
(C) 4
(D) 5

Go on to the next page

6. Which of the following would complete the picture above to make a rectangle?

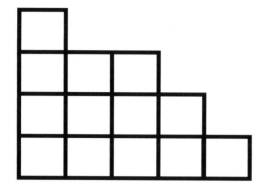

(A)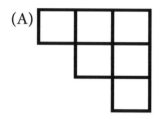

(B)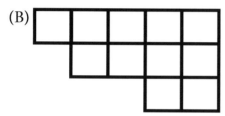

(C)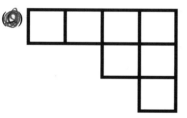

(D)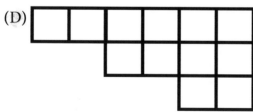

Go on to the next page

7. Liam and Harry were skiing at the same speed. It took Liam 24 minutes to ski 3 miles.
    How long did it take Harry to ski 9 miles?
    (A) 60 minutes
    (B) 72 minutes
    (C) 90 minutes
    (D) 96 minutes

8. Which fraction is greatest?
    (A) $\frac{6}{11}$
    (B) $\frac{7}{15}$
    (C) $\frac{8}{17}$
    (D) $\frac{9}{19}$

9. If w can be divided by both 2 and 3 with no remainder, then w can also be divided
    by which of the following and leave no remainder?
    (A) 4
    (B) 5
    (C) 6
    (D) 10

10. Using the Venn diagram below, which shape could be found in the shaded region of the
    diagram?

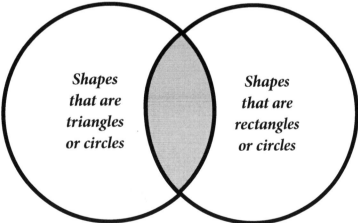

    (A) a red triangle
    (B) a green triangle
    (C) a blue rectangle
    (D) a yellow circle

Go on to the next page

11. What is the value of m in the equation $12 = 2m + 4$?
    (A) 1
    (B) 2
    (C) 4
    (D) 6

12. A class grew three different kinds of plants: grass, clover, and dandelions. They placed the plants in a sunny spot and measured their height each day. The table below shows the data that they collected.

HEIGHT OF PLANTS (in cm)			
	Grass	Clover	Dandelion
Day 1	1	1	0
Day 2	4	1	0
Day 3	6	2	1
Day 4	10	2	3
Day 5	13	3	6
Day 6	15	4	9

If the data continued to follow the same pattern, what would be the predicted height of the grass on Day 8?
    (A) 15 cm
    (B) 16 cm
    (C) 20 cm
    (D) 39 cm

Go on to the next page

13. Use the table below to answer the question.

Input ■	Output Δ
3	8
5	12
7	16
9	20

What rule does this function follow?
(A) $(■ \times 2) + 2 = Δ$
(B) $(■ \times 3) - 1 = Δ$
(C) $■ + 5 = Δ$
(D) $■ + 7 = Δ$

14. A triangle has three sides that are all the same length. If the perimeter of the triangle is $9k$, then what is the length of one side?
(A) 3
(B) 6
(C) $3k$
(D) $9k$

15. Use the equations to find the sum.

$4d + 5 = 17$
$3q = 15$

What is the sum of $d + q$?
(A) 3
(B) 5
(C) 7
(D) 8

Go on to the next page

16. Use the pattern below to answer the question.

Row 1 ●

Row 2 ● ●

Row 3 ● ● ●

Row 4 ● ● ● ●

The first four rows of a pattern are shown above. If this pattern is continued, how many dots would the sixth row have?

(A) 5

(B) 6

(C) 9

(D) 12

17. Which fraction is the least?

(A) $\frac{3}{7}$

(B) $\frac{5}{9}$

(C) $\frac{7}{12}$

(D) $\frac{8}{15}$

18. Use the pattern below to answer the question.

Julie creates a necklace using just black and white beads using the pattern shown above. The first bead is black, the second bead is white, the third and fourth beads are black, and so on. What number bead will the next black bead be?

(A) 1st

(D) 3rd

(C) 18th

(D) 21st

Go on to the next page

19. A survey asked 80 students what their favorite class was. The results are shown in the circle graph below.

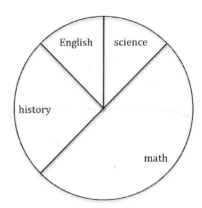

Approximately what fraction of the students said that science was their favorite class?
(A) $\frac{1}{2}$
(B) $\frac{1}{3}$
(C) $\frac{1}{4}$
(D) $\frac{1}{8}$

20. Sarah measured four lizards. She found that two lizards were each $3\frac{1}{2}$ inches long, another lizard was 4 inches long, and the final lizard was 5 inches long. What was the mean length of the lizards that Sarah measured?
(A) 3 inches
(B) $3\frac{1}{2}$ inches
(C) 4 inches
(D) 5 inches

21. To answer the question, use the following number line:

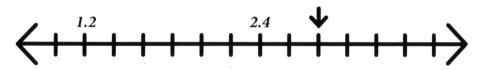

What number is the vertical arrow pointing to?
(A) 2.6
(B) 2.8
(C) 3.0
(D) 3.2

Go on to the next page

22. Use the figure below to answer the question.

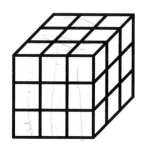

The larger cube above is made up of smaller cubes that are all the same size and shape. If the volume of each smaller cube is 1 unit³, what is the volume of the larger cube?
(A) 54 units³
(B) 27 units³
(C) 9 units³
(D) 3 units³

23. Use the picture below to answer the question.

L   M   N

The length of *LM* is *b* and the length of *MN* is *c*. What is the length of *LN*?
(A) bc
(B) $b - c$
(C) $c - b$
(D) $b + c$

24. A store has 472 boxes of pencils. There are 12 pencils in each box. The store manager wants to know about how many total pencils the store has. Which expression would give her the best estimate of the total number of pencils?
(A) 440×10
(B) 40×100
(C) 500×10
(D) 400×20

Go on to the next page

25. Two glasses each hold 1 cup of liquid. One glass is $2/3$ full and the other glass is $3/4$ full. If both glasses were poured into an empty pitcher, about how much liquid would be in that pitcher?

(A) $5/6$ cup

(B) 1 cup

(C) 1.5 cups

(D) 2 cups

26. Use the figure below to answer the question.

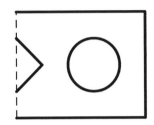

A piece of paper was folded along the dotted line as shown. A triangle and circle were then cut from the folded piece of paper, as shown. What will the piece of paper look like when it is unfolded?

(A)

(B)

(C)

(D)

Go on to the next page

27. To make a juice cocktail, the following juices were added into a pitcher:

   3 cups apple juice
   4 cups orange juice
   5 cups grapefruit juice
   2 cups cranberry juice
   2 cups grape juice

The juice cocktail was then evenly divided among six smaller cups. About how much juice cocktail did each cup contain?
   (A) 1 cup
   (B) 2 cups
   (C) 2.5 cups
   (D) 6 cups

28. The scale of a model airplane shows that 0.8 inches on the model airplane represents five feet on the actual airplane. If the model airplane is 3.2 inches long, then what is the length of the actual airplane?
   (A) 0.8 feet
   (B) 3.2 feet
   (C) 4 feet
   (D) 20 feet

29. There are blue and green marbles in a bag. The probability that a green marble will be drawn from the bag is 5 out of 9. If there are 12 blue marbles in the bag, how many green marbles are there?
   (A) 15
   (B) 18
   (C) 20
   (D) 27

Go on to the next page

30. Use the figure below to answer the question.

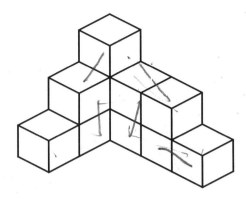

How many small cubes were used to build the figure above?

(A) 9

(B) 11

(C) 15

(D) 20

31. A class counted up the number of students on each of four buses. The graph below shows what the students found.

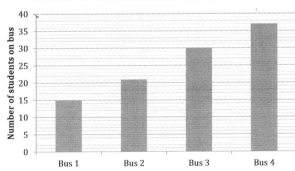

Based on the above graph, which of the following conclusions is true about the number of students on each bus?

(A) There are more students on Bus 1 than there are on Bus 4.

(B) The range is greater than the number of students on Bus 2.

(C) The mean is the same as the number of students on Bus 1.

(D) There are more students on Bus 3 than there are on Bus 1 and Bus 2 combined.

Go on to the next page

32. Which equation correctly represents the statement "3 less than twice a number is equal to six less than the number" if v represents the unknown number?
(A) $3 - (v \times 2) = 6 - v$
(B) $3 - (v \times 2) = v - 6$
(C) $(v \times 2) - 3 = 6 - v$
(D) $(v \times 2) - 3 = v - 6$

33. Use the figure below to answer the question.

How many lines of symmetry does the above figure have?
(A) 1
(B) 3
(C) 5
(D) 6

34. Maureen has a box of donuts. There are glazed, chocolate, vanilla, and sugared donuts in the box. The probability of choosing a glazed donut is 3 out of 7. Which combination of donuts is possible?
(A) 9 glazed donuts and 12 others
(B) 9 glazed donuts and 27 others
(C) 15 glazed donuts and 7 others
(D) 18 glazed donuts and 15 others

35. Use the expression below to answer the question.

$$\frac{39 \times 689}{20}$$

What is a reasonable estimate of the result of the above calculation?
(A) between 900 and 1100
(B) between 1100 and 1400
(C) between 1400 and 1800
(D) between 1800 and 2500

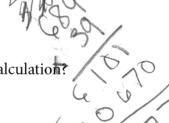

Go on to the next page

36. Use the equation below to answer the question.

$$\frac{5(45+5)}{10} = m$$

What is the value of m?
(A) 25
(B) 50
(C) 100
(D) 250

37. Use the number line below to answer the question.

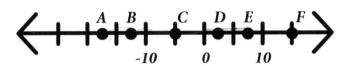

Point C is the average of A and another point. Which point represents that other number?
(A) B
(B) D
(C) E
(D) F

38. Use the figure below to answer the question.

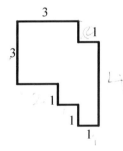

What is the perimeter of the figure above?
(A) 9
(B) 10
(C) 15
(D) 18

STOP. If you have time left, you may check your answers in ONLY this section.

Section 3—Reading Comprehension

25 questions
25 minutes

The Reading Comprehension section has five short passages. Each passage has five questions after it. Choose the answer choice that comes closest to what is stated or implied in the passage. You can write in the test booklet.

STOP. Do not move on to the section until told to.

Questions 1-5

1 Eleanor Roosevelt was born into a wealthy family in New York. She could have spent
2 her life living grandly. Instead, she chose to spend her time helping others defend their
3 rights.
4
5 When Eleanor was just 20 years old, she married Franklin D. Roosevelt. Franklin D.
6 Roosevelt would go on to be the president of the United States for four terms. This made
7 Eleanor Roosevelt the longest serving First Lady in the history of the United States. Before
8 Eleanor, First Ladies were mainly expected to entertain guests and help their husbands.
9
10 Eleanor had very different ideas about what a First Lady should do. Before the Roosevelts,
11 just the president would hold press conferences and speak at national conventions.
12
13 Eleanor Roosevelt did not see why she could not speak to the press. She started
14 holding her own press conferences to reach other Americans. In 1940, she also became
15 the first spouse of a president to speak at a national convention.
16
17 There were many causes that Eleanor Roosevelt cared very deeply about. She tried
18 to improve living conditions for the working class. In 1933 she went to Arthurdale,
19 West Virginia. While she was there she met miners who had lost their jobs and were
20 now homeless. She was deeply affected by this visit. It inspired her to set up a
21 community for the homeless miners.
22
23 She also fought for the rights of African-Americans. She protested that African-
24 Americans in the South were not receiving their fair share of federal money. She also
25 invited hundreds of African-Americans to the White House. This had never been done
26 before. The Daughters of the American Revolution would not let an African-American
27 singer perform at Constitution Hall. Eleanor Roosevelt heard this and arranged for the
28 concert to be given in front of the Lincoln Memorial.
29
30 During her lifetime, Eleanor Roosevelt was both criticized and greatly admired. She
31 fought for rapid change. This made her a lot of enemies. The groups of people that she
32 stood up for, however, will never forget her help. Eleanor Roosevelt was a woman who
33 sacrificed for what she thought was right.

Go on to the next page

1. The main purpose of this passage is to
   (A) explain how Eleanor Roosevelt's wealth affected her life.
   (B) discuss the role of women during Franklin D. Roosevelt's presidency.
   (C) analyze the importance of Arthurdale.
   (D) relate how Eleanor Roosevelt supported various causes.

2. The passage states that First Ladies before Eleanor Roosevelt
   (A) did not give press conferences.
   (B) frequently invited African-Americans to the White House.
   (C) performed in front of the Lincoln Memorial.
   (D) were concerned with workers' conditions.

3. In line 15, the word "spouse" means
   (A) president.
   (B) husband or wife.
   (C) worker.
   (D) entertainer.

4. According to the passage, how did other people view Eleanor Roosevelt?
   (A) She was adored by everyone who met her.
   (B) She was a controversial figure.
   (C) Many people did not know who she was.
   (D) She was just like the First Ladies that came before her.

5. The passage answers which of the following questions?
   (A) Who was the First Lady before Eleanor Roosevelt?
   (B) Did Eleanor Roosevelt belong to the Daughters of the American Revolution?
   (C) What state was Arthurdale located in?
   (D) Did Eleanor Roosevelt have any children?

Go on to the next page

Questions 6-10

1 Groucho Marx once said, "A black cat crossing your path signifies that the animal is
2 going somewhere." Groucho Marx did not believe that black cats are lucky or unlucky.
3 Many people would disagree, however.
4
5 In some cultures, black cats are considered good luck. In Great Britain, brides are given
6 black cat tokens by well-wishers. In Celtic myths, a good fairy takes the form of a black
7 cat. Black cats are also seen as lucky in Japan.
8
9 In Egypt, blacks cats were considered a way to gain the favor of the gods. The goddess Bast
10 was thought to like black cats. Families would have black cats in their homes in in order
11 to get on Bast's good side. In England, King Charles also thought that his black cat
12 would bring him good luck. He was arrested soon after his black cat died so perhaps he
13 had a point.
14
15 Other cultures believe that black cats bring harm. The Pilgrims believed that anyone with
16 a black cat was a witch. In southern and western Europe, many people think that black
17 cats are evil. During the Middle Ages this belief brought disaster to Europe. Cats hunt
18 rodents that spread disease. Many black cats were killed during the Middle Ages and
19 this allowed the rat population to increase. More rats meant more disease, such as the
20 plague.
21
22 Some cultures view black cats as both lucky and unlucky. In Germany, if a black cat
23 crosses your path from left to right it is a good sign. If the cat crosses your path right
24 to left it is a bad sign. In the 1700s, pirates also had their own ideas about black cats.
25 They believed that a cat walking toward a person is good luck. A cat walking away from
26 a person would bring bad luck.
27
28 Whether or not black cats bring good or bad luck is not certain. Either way, black cats
29 have not gone unnoticed.

Go on to the next page

6. The main idea of this passage is
   (A) Halloween traditions.
   (B) the future of black cats.
   (C) the importance of folklore in Egypt.
   (D) what people from different cultures think about black cats.

7. According to the passage, what do Great Britain and Egypt have in common?
   (A) Their citizens do not trust black cats.
   (B) There are no black cats in either country.
   (C) Their citizens consider black cats to be lucky.
   (D) Their citizens believe that sometimes black cats are good luck and sometimes they
       are bad luck.

8. In line 1, the word "signifies" most nearly means
   (A) represents.
   (B) discovers.
   (C) leaves.
   (D) crowds.

9. According to the passage, Groucho Marx believed which of the following?
   (A) Black cats are to be avoided.
   (B) A person should not place importance on the fact that a black cat has walked in front
       of them.
   (C) Black cats have a long tradition in many cultures.
   (D) Cats are an important part of society.

10. Which statement about cats is supported by the passage?
    (A) Their population has grown recently.
    (B) They are not allowed in certain countries.
    (C) They usually bring good luck.
    (D) They sometimes hunt rats which can help to reduce certain diseases.

Go on to the next page

Questions 11-15

1 Danger was building in New York and its citizens were in quiet suspense and fearful
2 anticipation. In Philadelphia, the General Congress was discussing what John Adams
3 called, "The greatest question ever debated in America, and as great as ever was or will
4 be discussed among men." The result was a resolution passed unanimously on the 2nd of
5 July - "that these United Colonies are, and of right need to be, free and independent
6 States."

7

8 "The 2nd of July," added John Adams, "will be the most memorable date in the history of
9 America. I do believe that it will be celebrated by future generations as the great
10 anniversary of our freedom… It should be celebrated with cheer and parade, with shows,
11 games, sports, guns, bells, bonfires, and fireworks, from one end of this nation to the
12 other, from this time forth."

13

14 The signing of that declaration has given rise to an annual jubilee, but not on the day
15 named by Adams. The Fourth of July is when the United States celebrates its freedom,
16 not the second of July. For a long time, it was believed that the Declaration of Independence
17 was actually signed on the Fourth of July, so that is the day that is celebrated.

18

19 More recently, however, some scholars have cast serious doubt on the claim that the
20 Declaration of Independence was signed on the Fourth of July. It is now believed that
21 the document wasn't even signed by all of the state representatives at the same time. Most
22 of the delegates probably signed it on Aug. 2. However, it was not even until August 30
23 that the British government in London knew that America had declared independence.

Go on to the next page

11. The primary purpose of this passage is to
    (A) explain why John Adams did not tell the truth.
    (B) explore the causes that led to the Declaration of Independence.
    (C) correct a misunderstanding about the Fourth of July.
    (D) discuss how historians discovered an error.

12. The passage states that what happened on the second of July?
    (A) A resolution was passed for independence in Philadelphia.
    (B) There were riots in New York.
    (C) The Declaration of Independence was signed.
    (D) The British government learned that America had declared independence.

13. In line 14, "jubilee" most nearly means
    (A) declaration.
    (B) celebration.
    (C) signing.
    (D) pen.

14. The passage implies that
    (A) independence was not a goal of American citizens.
    (B) not all of the delegates voted for independence.
    (C) John Adams was the first signer of the Declaration of Independence.
    (D) there was no one signing ceremony where all of the delegates signed the declaration.

15. Which of the following questions is answered by the passage?
    (A) Did John Adams sign the Declaration of Independence?
    (B) What city was the General Congress held in?
    (C) What was Britain's reaction to the Declaration of Independence?
    (D) How many signers were there of the Declaration of Independence?

Go on to the next page

Question 16–20

1 Not too long ago, people threw everything into the garbage. Landfills were filling up too
2 quickly. Now we recycle glass, metal, paper, and many other materials that used to go
3 in the trash. Many cities and towns are now turning their attention to yard and food
4 waste. When we rake leaves, we can put them in garbage bags and take them to the
5 dump. If the leaves are in plastic bags, buried in a pile of trash, they take up space. But
6 leaves and grass clippings can be put to better use. Yard waste can be composted.
7
8 Composting helps return yard waste to nature. Leaves, grass, and food scraps can be
9 turned into fertilizer. People with gardens can have their own compost bins. Gardeners
10 can wait for the materials to break down on their own, or they can help move the process
11 along. Allowing worms into the compost bin is one method. The worms eat the leaves
12 and other matter, helping to break it down into usable soil.
13
14 The materials that should be composted can vary. Many cities with curbside yard waste
15 collection allow any kind of food. They also allow compostable food packaging, which is
16 becoming more common. Most backyard compost bins are not designed for meat and
17 dairy waste. These foods will smell bad and attract pests if they are not disposed of
18 properly. Also, putting certain things into the compost bin might lead to a surprise. If
19 you toss some old pumpkins into the compost bin after Halloween, the seeds may begin
20 to sprout and create a pumpkin patch!
21
22 It is amazing to see how little garbage we generate when we recycle and compost. A
23 family of four may produce only one medium-sized bag of garbage per week. By helping
24 us to reduce the waste we send to the landfill, composting can have a greater impact than
25 we realize.

Go on to the next page

16. The main idea of the passage is best expressed by which of the following?
    (A) Composting can significantly reduce waste that winds up in the landfill.
    (B) Worms can be used to speed along composting.
    (C) Families produce too much garbage.
    (D) Recycling is now more common.

17. In the third paragraph (lines 14-20), the author implies that
    (A) composting is becoming more common.
    (B) neighborhood associations might object to composting.
    (C) citywide composting generally allows for a greater variety of materials to be composted than backyard composting.
    (D) a compost bin is the best place to start seedlings.

18. The function of the last paragraph (lines 22-25) is to
    (A) provide a suspenseful ending so that readers will continue to research composting.
    (B) disprove a common argument.
    (C) provide evidence that composting is easily done.
    (D) remind the reader of the positive impact of composting.

19. Which word best characterizes composting as it is explained in the passage?
    (A) disgusting
    (B) beneficial
    (C) crowded
    (D) unusual

20. In line 22, the word "generate" most nearly means
    (A) create.
    (B) reduce.
    (C) confirm.
    (D) lose.

Go on to the next page

Questions 21–25

1 I took a group of students to the Seattle Public Library to see not only the books and
2 other materials in the collection, but also the art and architecture of the building itself.
3 Some of the students wanted to look out at the city from the tenth-floor viewpoint. On
4 the fifth floor, we got on a set of bright yellow escalators heading up. When we reached
5 the seventh floor, we walked across the hallway to the second escalator, which would
6 take us the rest of the way. When we arrived at the top, one of the students, Marco, was
7 missing.
8
9 I told the students who were still with me to stay on the tenth floor. Under no
10 circumstances were they to come looking for me, because then they might get lost, too.
11 Guessing that Marco had gotten distracted on the seventh floor, I rode down to find him.
12 One of the interesting features of the library is that the sixth through ninth floors are
13 built in an enormous spiral, with bookshelves lining the walls. As I passed the eighth
14 floor heading down, I saw Marco on the spiral walking up. I considered calling out to
15 him but stopped myself. If he saw me going down, would he turn around and follow me?
16 If he saw me going down but pointing for him to keep going up, would he understand
17 my plan?
18
19 I decided to keep quiet, ride the escalator to the seventh floor, and then ride back up to
20 the tenth floor and wait for Marco to arrive. When he did, out of breath and ready to
21 protest, I gave him a look. He swallowed hard, gave me a weak smile, and joined his
22 classmates at the windows.

Go on to the next page

21. This passage is primarily about
    (A) the floorplan of the Seattle library.
    (B) how to plan a fieldtrip.
    (C) an experience that a teacher had.
    (D) why Marco got a low grade on his trip notebook.

22. In line 21, the word "protest" most nearly means
    (A) complain.
    (B) listen.
    (C) leave.
    (D) discard.

23. It can be inferred from the passage that
    (A) the teacher frequently had trouble with Marco.
    (B) Marco was very out of shape.
    (C) fieldtrips are important.
    (D) the architecture of the Seattle Library is unusual.

24. According to the passage, the teacher did not call out to Marco because
    (A) she was afraid that Marco would not hear her.
    (B) she thought Marco might turn around and get further lost.
    (C) she didn't want the other students to know that Marco was missing.
    (D) she didn't see Marco.

25. Which question is answered by information in the passage?
    (A) How many floors does the Seattle Library have?
    (B) How many students were on the fieldtrip?
    (C) What grade were the students in?
    (D) What color was the escalator?

STOP. If you have time left, you may check your answers in ONLY this section.

Section 4—Mathematics Achievement

30 questions

30 minutes

Each math question has four answer choices after it. Choose the answer choice that best answers the question.

Make sure that you fill in the correct answer on your answer sheet. You may write in the test booklet.

SAMPLE QUESTION:

1. Which number can be divided by 4 with nothing left over?
   (A) 6
   (●) 12
   (C) 15
   (D) 22

Since 12 can be divided by 4 with no remainder, circle B is filled in.

STOP. Do not move on to the section until told to.

1. Use the rectangle below to answer this question.

5 inches

4 inches

What is the perimeter of the rectangle?
$(P = s + s + s + s)$

(A) 9 inches
(B) 10 inches
(C) 18 inches
(D) 24 inches

2. There are a total of 26 animals at the animal shelter. There are only dogs, cats, and rabbits at the animal shelter. If there are 14 dogs and 8 cats, how many rabbits are there?
(A) 4
(B) 5
(C) 9
(D) 22

3. What is the name of a shape that has five sides?
(A) hexagon
(B) pentagon
(C) rectangle
(D) triangle

4. Which of the following is the number four hundred thirteen thousand three hundred and nine written in standard form?
(A) 403, 390
(B) 403, 039
(C) 413, 039
(D) 413, 309

Go on to the next page

5. Use the following number line to answer this question.

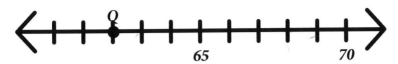

What number does point Q represent?
(A) 60
(B) 62
(C) 64
(D) 67

6. What is the value of the sum 289 + 117?
(A) 306
(B) 389
(C) 406
(D) 416

7. What is the value of the expression 4 × (3 + 6) − 5?
(A) 13
(B) 31
(C) 36
(D) 42

8. Sarah asked 24 classmates whether they preferred hot dogs, hamburgers, or neither. If 12 people told her they preferred hot dogs, and 7 people told her that they preferred neither one, how many people said that they preferred hamburgers?
(A) 5
(B) 7
(C) 9
(D) 12

Go on to the next page

9. A restaurant sells pizza, salad, and hamburgers. For one week, the restaurant owner made a chart showing how many of each type of food she sold during that day. The chart is given below.

NUMBER OF MENU ITEMS SOLD			
	Pizza	**Salad**	**Hamburgers**
Sunday	35	20	17
Monday	26	42	25
Tuesday	31	34	41
Wednesday	27	41	15
Thursday	34	51	42
Friday	17	32	45
Saturday	19	15	42

On Thursday, how many more salads were sold than hamburgers?
(A) 3
(B) 5
(C) 8
(D) 9

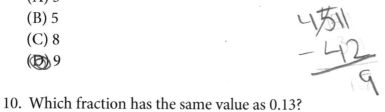

10. Which fraction has the same value as 0.13?
(A) $\frac{1}{13}$
(B) $\frac{1}{130}$
(C) $\frac{13}{10}$
(D) $\frac{13}{100}$

11. Which decimal number is equivalent to $\frac{3}{10}$?
(A) 3.0
(B) 0.3
(C) 0.03
(D) 0.003

Go on to the next page

12. Which of the following is equivalent to 3,000 − 255?
    (A) 2,545
    (B) 2,645
    (C) 2,745
    (D) 2,845

13. In the equation $3 \times (\Delta + 5) = 21$, what number should replace Δ in order to make the equation true?
    (A) 1
    (B) 2
    (C) 5
    (D) 7

14. Carol bought 8 balloons, each of which cost 65 cents. What is the estimated total cost for the eight balloons?
    (A) between $5.00 and $5.50
    (B) between $5.50 and $6.00
    (C) between $6.00 and $6.50
    (D) between $6.50 and $7.00

15. Josh bought four items. These four items cost $0.99, $3.49, $4.75, and $6.25. He wants to make sure that he has enough money so he estimates what the total cost will be. What is the correct estimate?
    (A) between $15 and $16
    (B) between $16 and $17
    (C) between $17 and $18
    (D) between $18 and $19

Go on to the next page

16. The graph below shows the number of books in a classroom library.

BOOKS IN A CLASSROOM LIBRARY	
History	
English	
Science	
Math	

= 200 books

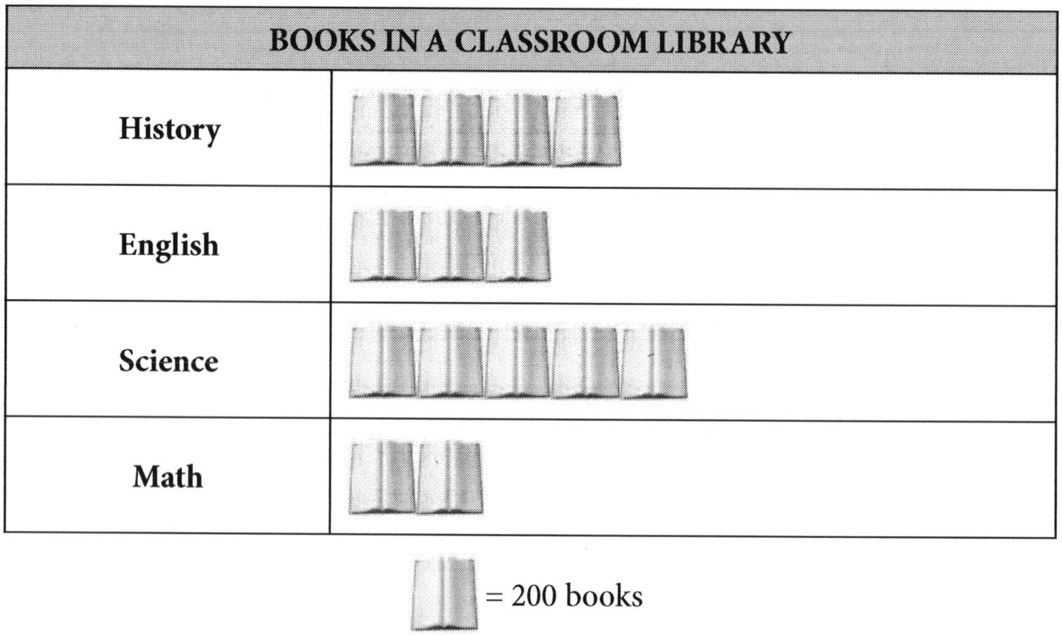

How many more science books are there than math books?
(A) 3
(B) 200
(C) 600
(D) 1,000

17. The town of Smithville has a population of about 29,821 people. Which town has a population closest to $\frac{1}{4}$ that of Smithville?
(A) Janestown, which has a population of 7,645
(B) Clearmont, which has a population of 8,742
(C) Henryville, which has a population of 15,914
(D) Greyburg, which has a population of 22,871

18. Thirteen cards, numbered 1 through 13, are placed facedown on a table. If a card is randomly picked, what is the chance that an odd number will be on that card?
(A) 1 out of 2
(B) 1 out of 13
(C) 6 out of 13
(D) 7 out of 13

Go on to the next page

19. Ms. Hamill's class made a table of their test scores on the last five tests.

	Test 1	Test 2	Test 3	Test 4
Sam	79	91	85	79
Lisa	81	85	90	91
Jack	85	79	86	95
Mimi	79	86	91	70

What is the mode of their test scores?
(A) 70
(B) 79
(C) 81
(D) 85

20. Use the following set of numbers to answer the question.

$\{4, 6, 21, 45, 60\}$

Which term describes all the numbers in this set?
(A) even numbers
(B) odd numbers
(C) composite numbers
(D) prime numbers

21. The area of a certain triangle is 30 cm². Which equation can be used to find the base of that triangle? ($A = \frac{1}{2}bh$, where A = Area, b = length of base, and h = height of triangle)
(A) $b = \frac{30}{h}$
(B) $b = 30h$
(C) $b = \frac{60}{h}$
(D) $b = 60h$

Go on to the next page

22. Which of the following fractions is between $\frac{1}{6}$ and $\frac{1}{2}$?
    (A) $\frac{3}{7}$
    (B) $\frac{4}{7}$
    (C) $\frac{7}{9}$
    (D) $\frac{9}{10}$

23. Use the following number sequence.

    3, 6, 10, 15, 21, ■

    What number should replace the ■?
    (A) 22
    (B) 24
    (C) 27
    (D) 28

24. If it is 9 AM in Washington, D.C., it is 6 AM in San Francisco. An airplane takes off from Washington, D.C., at 12 noon and lands in San Francisco five hours later. What time is it in San Francisco when the airplane lands?
    (A) 7 AM
    (B) 2 PM
    (C) 5 PM
    (D) 8 PM

25. What is the difference of 7.2 − 1.9?
    (A) 5.2
    (B) 5.3
    (C) 6.2
    (D) 9.1

26. What is the perimeter of a square that has side lengths of 6 cm? ($P = 4s$)
    (A) 8 cm
    (B) 16 cm
    (C) 24 cm
    (D) 28 cm

Go on to the next page

27. Use the following coordinate grid to answer the question

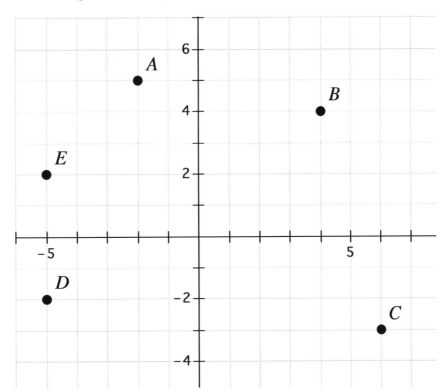

Which point has the coordinates (−5, 2)?
(A) A
(B) C
(C) D
(D) E

28. Which mixed number is equivalent to 1.4 + 2.8?
(A) $3\frac{4}{5}$
(B) $4\frac{1}{5}$
(C) $4\frac{2}{5}$
(D) $4\frac{4}{5}$

29. Which of the following is a prime number?
(A) 2
(B) 4
(C) 9
(D) 12

Go on to the next page

30. Larry had $3\frac{5}{6}$ feet of rope. He gave Mark $2\frac{1}{3}$ feet of that rope. How many feet of rope does Larry have left?

(A) $1\frac{1}{3}$

(B) $1\frac{1}{2}$

(C) $2\frac{1}{3}$

(D) $2\frac{2}{3}$

STOP. If you have time left, you may check your answers in ONLY this section.

Essay

You will be given 30 minutes to plan and write an essay. The topic is printed on the next page. *Make sure that you write about this topic. Do NOT choose another topic.*

This essay gives you the chance to show your thinking and how well you can express your ideas. Do not worry about filling all of the space provided. The quality is more important than how much you write. You should probably write more than a brief paragraph, though.

A copy of this essay will be sent to the schools that you apply to. Make sure that you only write in the appropriate area on the answer sheet. Please print so that the admissions officers can understand what you wrote.

On the next page is the topic sheet. There is room on this sheet to make notes and collect your thoughts. The final essay should be written on the two lined sheets provided in the answer sheet, however. Make sure that you copy your topic at the top of the first lined page. Write only in blue or black ink.

REMINDER: Please remember to write the topic on the top of the first lined page in your answer sheet.

> Who do you most admire? Why do you admire this person?

- Write only about this topic
- Only the lined sheets will be sent to schools
- Use only blue or black ink

Notes

_____

_____

_____

_____

_____

_____

_____

_____

_____

_____